BIZARRE BUT TRUE

BLITZ EDITIONS

Published by Blitz Editions
an imprint of Bookmart Ltd
Registered Number 2372865
Trading as Bookmart Ltd, Desford Road, Enderby
Leicester LE9 5AD

This book was produced
by Amazon Publishing Ltd

Cover design: Peter Dolton
Text design: Jim Reader
Production Manager: Sue Gray
Editorial Manager: Roz Williams

Printed in the Slovak Republic
51735

ISBN 1 85605 204 4

This material has previously appeared in *Fated Destiny*.

Every effort has been made to contact the copyright holders for the pictures. In some cases they have been untraceable, for which we offer our apologies. Thanks to the Hulton Deutsch Collection Ltd, who supplied most of them.
Pictures have been provided as follows: Janet & Colin Bord (p 23), E P A Photo Library (p 12 bottom), Mary Evans (pp 32, 33 top, 34, 35 top, 42, 50), Fortean Picture Library (pp 21, 22), Hulton Deutsch Collection Ltd (pp 3, 6 top, 9 top, 11–16, 19, 22 bottom, 24, 26, 28, 33 bottom, 34 top, 35 bottom–40, 47 bottom, 55–57, 59, 66, 77 top), Mander & Mitchenson Theatre Collection (pp 43, 45, 46, 51 right), Press Association Photo Library (pp 63, 68, 70, 71), Peter Newark's American Pictures (pp 18, 44), Peter Newark's Historical Pictures (pp 27, 29–31, 43 top, 52, 53), Peter Newark's Western Americana (p 49), Popperfoto (pp 2, 4, 5, 6 bottom, 7 bottom, 17), Portfolio (pp 62, 64, 65, 67, 69), Rex Features (pp 8, 9 bottom, 10, 11 top, 14, 41, 79, 80), Syndication International (pp 25, 54, 60, 61).

Cover: The main, front left and right pictures supplied by the Hulton Deutsch Collection Ltd. The centre by Rex Features. The back cover picture supplied by the Hulton Deutsch Collection Ltd.

The Authors

Karen Farrington is a journalist who has worked for both national newspapers, and as a freelance, for the best selling weekly women's magazines. Her broad experience has brought her into contact with some of the most intriguing mysteries, compelling crimes and moving animal stories of recent times.

Nick Constable, also a journalist, has spent many years working in Fleet Street and covered top stories including the famine in Ethiopia, the government-backed assassinations of street children in Brazil and the Gulf War. He has also worked extensively to expose cruelty to animals in Britain and around the world.

BIZARRE BUT TRUE

JIM JONES AND DAVID KORESH
Mad messiahs

Every few years a new 'messiah' appears on the scene, seducing the desperate and the gullible with promises of a new life on Earth and heavenly salvation. Too often their faith is rewarded only with destruction and the most hideous deaths.

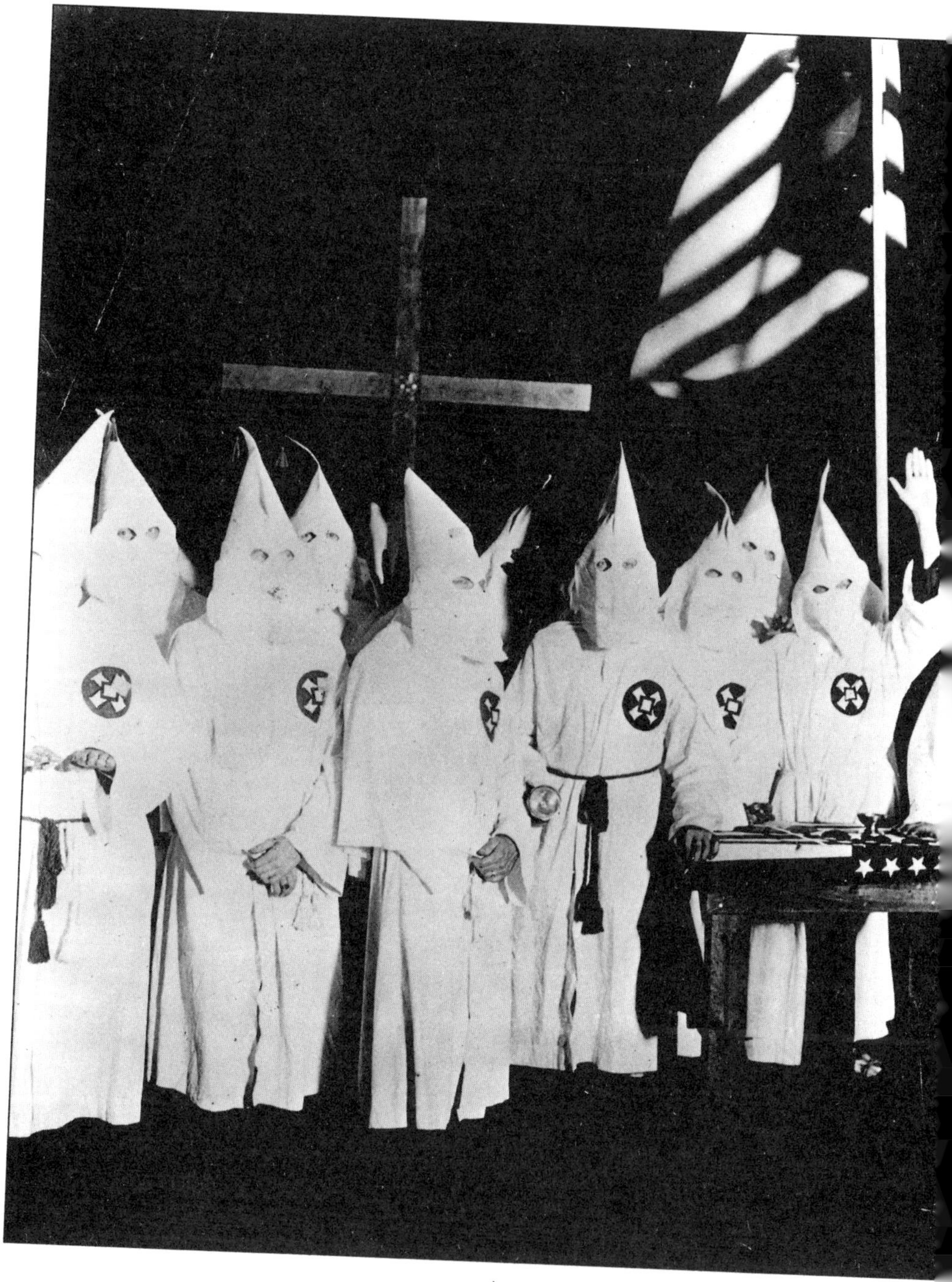

In their minds, his disciples believed the Rev Jim Jones was a saviour who would lead them to harmony and happiness.

In reality, Jones was a power-crazed zealot with scant regard for the well-being of his followers. When his earthly empire started to crumble he led almost 1,000 people to their deaths in an astonishing mass suicide rather than face disgrace and condemnation from the rest of the world.

On his orders, the people he had united at a jungle settlement in Guyana willingly slurped arsenic poisoning. His triumphal cries were ringing in their ears. 'We were too good for this world. Now come with me and I will take you to a better place.'

Jim Jones was the only, lonely child of a World War 1 veteran and a Cherokee Indian woman. His father, suffering a lung disease as a result of his service, was unable to work and survived on a paltry pension. He searched for a scapegoat for his woes and found it in the form of the country's black population. To young Jim's horror, he backed the racist Ku Klux Klan.

PULPIT POWER

To escape the shame he felt at his father's extremism, Jim immersed himself in religion. His first taste of 'pulpit power' was when he stood on the step outside his suburban home and preached the gospel to passers-by. He was 12 years old.

Jones was already deeply involved in religion and was intent on making it his life's work. He took a Bible studies course at Indiana University, working as a hospital porter to finance the extra learning. It was here he met his future wife Marceline Baldwin, a nurse four years his senior, with whom he adopted seven children from various ethnic backgrounds.

His next step was to become a pastor in an Indianapolis church, which meant first-hand experience of crossing the race divide. He was gratified to discover the faith and support he commanded among his congregation when he clashed with the bigots who wanted to keep blacks out of the church.

Above: ***Masked and robed, the Ku Klux Klan sought to cow and kill black people living in America. To his horror, Jim Jones found his father was an active supporter of the menacing and sinister movement.***

Opposite: ***Hundreds of devotees of Jim Jones drank poisoned cordial from a trough to die alongside their leader. Waverers were persuaded to down the spiked potion at the point of a gun.***

people who sat enthralled through his compelling sermons drew together in fierce support of the man they considered their leader.

He had a dream, a vision of a socialist community where people would work for the good of others, seeking not to better their bank balance but improve their souls. He sincerely yearned to lead a peaceful colony in which brotherhood and humanity were paramount. Sadly, his ideas became warped along the way.

Once again, toying with the strength of his followers' beliefs, he branched out into faith healing. It was accompanied with all his usual flourish and showmanship but for the first time, he ventured into the realms of deceit. Among the sick and crippled people who queued up to see him were decoys from his most trusted disciples. While the genuinely sick people remained unmoved by his theatrical hands-on healing, the frauds would rise and claim they had been miraculously cured. Cruelly, he claimed he could cure cancer. In reality, the hapless victims were taken into the toilet by his wife Marceline who produced a mouldy chicken's liver in a piece of tissue claiming it was the obnoxious tumour. Jones also claimed he could raise the dead. It was a tempting lure for the old and the sick.

Above: ***Pictured in 1976, the Rev Jim Jones looked clean cut and dapper. Neighbours were impressed with the charitable works carried out by Jones and his supporters. There was little to indicate that he was a budding sex maniac and sadist who would bed women, girls and even men to satisfy his enormous appetite. No one suspected he would start torturing children with electric cattle prods and administer savage beatings.***

He cautiously gauged the feelings of this new-found flock. Would they help him build his dream, a church for all races and creeds?

He discovered that he could exact money from them with relative ease. The People's Temple was duly built on the wrong side of the tracks in Indianapolis.

It was a mainly black congregation and Jones quickly assumed the style of the flamboyant coloured preachers who ranted, sang, whispered and bellowed with enormous dramatic effect.

Jones had already learned how people would unite behind him in the face of adversity. With this in mind, he publicized how he was the victim of a race hate campaign which included dynamite being thrown in his garden and a bottle being smashed in his face. As he expected, the

AN IDEAL COMMUNITY?

However, it was a dangerous ruse and Jones knew it. Before too long the state authorities and probing newspapers would be ready to expose his antics as phony. In a bold move, Jones planned the departure of himself and his trusting band to California's Redwood Valley where they could live in peace among other hippy drop-outs of the age.

On the face of it, the People's Temple was everything a community could wish for. Members were always ready to lend a hand, be it on local farms or as foster parents or in charity work. Jones himself worked tirelessly to secure local positions of political power, including the foreman of the county grand jury and a director of free legal aid services. Local police forces received donations for the widow and orphans' fund, while newspapers won cash awards for printing 'outstanding journalistic contributions to peace and public enlightenment'. By 1976 Jones was the picture of respectability when he was photographed rubbing shoulders with Rosalynn Carter, the campaigning wife of presidential hopeful Jimmy. He even received an invitation to the subsequent inauguration ceremony in Washington. With the opening of a new Temple in San Francisco, thousands more were recruited to his cause. Soon there was another Temple opened in Los Angeles. Jones decided the big city was a better hunting ground and based his whole operation there.

But behind the scenes there were sinister undertones. By now Jones, with his dyed black hair and sunglasses which never left his nose, had perverted most of his lauded principles to satisfy an egoistical mania. Disciples were told to hand over their earnings and savings and this meant the coffers of his degenerating organization were overflowing.

More worryingly, Jones appeared to have embarked on a licentious campaign, using his position of authority to bed any woman or girl he chose. Marriages were broken up and Jones appointed himself as the arbitrator for future matches. He chose the most desirable women as wives for his trusted church elders. Equally, he enjoyed intimate relations with men. All the men who joined the church were publicly humiliated for their own sexual mores. Adults judged by large assemblies to need punishment were pitted in a boxing match against one or more stronger, fitter opponents to take a beating.

Children were thrashed and tortured with an electric cattle prod. Inevitably, there were those whom Jones could not control who were shocked and disillusioned by the excesses of Jones and his cohorts. Gradually word began to spread that the People's Temple was not the golden haven it appeared to be. Officials were reluctant to believe the man who did so much work for the community was a crook and a pervert, but the dribble of bad publicity grew into a flood and was hard to ignore.

When the cracks in his American operation started to show, Jones once again took the actions of a desperado. He uprooted the movement he had moulded, this time to the struggling republic of Guyana.

HE CLAIMED HE COULD REMOVE CANCEROUS TUMOURS – THE 'PROOF' WAS A MOULDY CHICKEN'S LIVER WRAPPED IN TOILET PAPER.

Below: ***Supporters flocked to the People's Temples launched by Jones in America. His sermons held their rapt attention. They were astonished at his ability to heal the sick. Little did they know as they handed over the cash they had that Jones was a faker who used actors in the audience when performing 'miracles'. Once they were in the clutches of the eerie Jones it was hard to escape. This picture was taken by Greg Robinson, one of three pressmen to be killed by Jones's henchmen at Jonestown.***

In the new, 'just' society the brainwashed disciples were forced to slave from dawn to dusk, and any protests were swiftly silenced by armed guards.

BRAINWASHED

He was, he told his people, setting up 'a new, just socialist society'. A thousand of his followers, by now brainwashed and unquestioning, went with him, handing over their passports 'for safe keeping' after they arrived. Their new home, called 'Jonestown', was patrolled by armed guards, apparently to defend the residents from bandits. But it was not the Shangri-la they were led to expect. They had to work from dawn until nightfall on a diet of rice and onions. Those deemed to be slacking in their work or doubting the wisdom of the leader were put in a tiny box where they would have to stay for days at a time. Children were led through the dark corridors of the jungle to a well where they would be dunked in time after time, shrieking in terror.

Cult devotees might have lived out their days in a twisted Utopia if the growing scandal about their activities hadn't pursued them to the jungle. US Congressman Leo Ryan was concerned enough about what he had heard from anxious constituents to investigate the sect himself.

Taking with him a TV crew, Congressman Ryan flew down to Jonestown. Once there, he told stunned disciples: 'If any of you want to leave, you can come with me under my personal guarantee of protection.'

Incredibly, despite the picture of Jones glowering over the assembly, one person plucked up enough courage to choose escape from the tyranny, then another. It was late, there would be no return home to the US that night. Suspicious of what might happen during darkness to those who wanted to leave, Ryan offered to stay at Jonestown while the TV crew spent the night in the nearest town some six miles away. Away from Jonestown, one of the TV reporters discovered a note in his pocket signed by four people which read: 'Please, please get us out of here before Jones kills us.'

But the full story of why devotees

Popular Congressman Leo Ryan (above) *was known for his forthright approach and no-nonsense attitude. He vowed to investigate claims of abuse at Jonestown. Ryan begged cult member Brian Bouquette* (right) *to speak to his mother – but in vain. The next day, he was among 911 people who took poison rather than face the condemnation of the outside world.*

Parents forced their babies to sup the cordial laced with poison.

Left: ***Father, mother and son lie in a last loving embrace. If the children were too small to drink from a cup, their parents used syringes to squirt the deadly squash into their mouths.***

Below: ***Larry Layton, 32, was one of Jones's trusted lieutenants. He asked to 'escape' Jonestown with Congressman Ryan. When a group of cult members tried to flee, he was among them and fired a hidden gun. He even tried to shoot the pilot of the rescue plane sent in. Later he was charged on five counts of murder and three of attempted murder in Jonestown.***

suddenly sought escape from the master would never be known. The extent of the power-mad frenzy displayed by Jones to those who once loved him will remain a secret for ever.

For when the journalists returned to collect Ryan and the 20 people who by then had decided to leave, a violent carnage began. One loyal follower lunged at Ryan with a knife, slashing himself in the process.

The journalists hauled Ryan onto the truck which was waiting to take them to the aircraft. But as they fled a tractor with armed assassins aboard trundled towards them. In a blast of gunfire, Ryan, a TV reporter and cameraman, a newspaper photographer and a fleeing cult member were all horribly killed. The survivors huddled together and tended each others' terrible wounds, receiving help from terrified locals who revealed aid was hours away.

Jones knew the end had come for him also. He gathered his people around him for the last time and urged them to drink the cordial he offered them that had already been laced with poison. Gun-toting church elders were on hand to make sure his will was done.

Even babes in arms were to die: their parents administered the noxious squash with a syringe. Amid failing choruses of gospel songs, the scores of faithful collapsed and died. Finally, a gunshot rang out. The Rev Jim Jones, 47, fell dead with a bullet in his head. The next day, 19 November 1978, Guyanese troops found the macabre scene of death and discovered whole families cold in a last, loving embrace.

Above: ***An inferno engulfed the compound at Waco after a 51-day seige, killing 87 followers of self-professed messiah David Koresh. Small children were among the dead. America watched in horror as the flames ripped through the Branch Davidian headquarters, fanned by the wind. Controversy still rages about what sparked the deadly blaze.***

THE WACO TRAGEDY

In the eighties, Vernon Howell was known to few outside his family and friends.

But by 1993 his name and face were splashed across every newspaper in the world. For Vernon Howell became David Koresh, the crazed leader of a sinister sect who died with 86 disciples in a fireball following a seven-week siege. Only nine people escaped when his headquarters at Waco, Texas, was set ablaze. Children and their mothers were among the dead.

The tragedy of such a senseless loss of life sent shock waves around the globe. There was horror that another quasi-messiah had taken control of the lives of so many; and anger that an early attempt to end the siege degenerated into a bloody shoot out. Finally, the watching world was sickened by the slaughter captured on TV cameras as the FBI moved in.

Vernon Wayne Howell was born in 1959 in Houston, Texas. His mum was just 15. Bonnie Clark, who worked in a nursing home, never married his 20-year-old carpenter father, Bobby Howell. The couple split up when Vernon was 2 years old.

Bonnie married Roy Haldeman and moved to a suburb of Dallas, but there was friction at home when young Vernon clashed with his stepfather. His hobby was reading the Bible and by the time he was 12, he had memorized the New Testament. His mother recalled how he would pray daily for long periods. 'I've seen him sitting by his bed on his knees for hours, crying and praying,' she said. 'Vernon was always a good boy.'

Despite his fervour for religious studies,

he dropped out of high school in 1977. He wanted to be a rock musician. If only he had succeeded, all those people who perished on 19 April 1993 when Waco burned might still be alive today.

When the dream of fame from guitar-strumming faded Howell looked for a new way to achieve fame for himself. Whether he planned for the infamy and notoriety now inextricably linked to his name, no one knows.

He became a member of the Seventh Day Adventist Church, being formally baptized into the faith when he was 20. The religious movement was founded in the last century on the firm belief in the Second Coming as described in the Bible's Revelation of St John. Its preaching also includes dire warnings of earthly disasters before the Son of God returns. It is particularly strong in America and the Caribbean.

But the peace-loving movement was not feisty enough for Howell. He was expelled by the time he was 22 when church elders realized his interpretation of the Bible was both radical and dubious. He was, they considered, a bad influence on the young.

By 1981 he alighted on the Branch Davidians, a group of disaffected Seventh Day Adventists who were based in Mount Carmel, in the farming heartland of Waco, Texas. It divided from the Seventh Day Adventists in the 1930s under the leadership of Victor Houteff, a Bulgarian born Adventist and, ironically, a confirmed pacifist. At the time Howell joined, it was led by Lois Roden, who was in her sixties.

THE BRUTAL MESSIAH

There followed a bizarre sequence of events which gives an early indication of Howell's disturbed state of mind. Although a humble handyman when he joined, his influence and power over the Branch Davidians mushroomed. He was showered with money taken out of the savings and pay packets of loyal followers living in San Bernadino, California. Some say he became Roden's lover. What is certain is that he and her son George fell out in spectacular style.

Howell was already calling himself a messiah, much to George's fury. In a macabre episode, George dug up a corpse from the local cemetery and challenged

Above: ***Americans were shocked that a cult leader had once again taken control of the lives of so many – and once again led those misguided followers to their doom. In sight of the charred remains of the Koresh stronghold, Rhiannon Gardner of California and Linda Caliva of San Diego put up crosses in memory of those cult members slaughtered in the fire and the four ATF agents who died in the original raid.***

Left: ***David Koresh, pictured here with his mother Bonnie and younger brother, was just like any other fresh-faced American boy. But after falling out with his stepfather, Vernon Howell – as he was known then – threw himself into religious studies. By the time he was 12 he had learned the entire New Testament off by heart.***

HE DUG UP THE ROTTING CORPSE AND CHALLENGED HIS MOTHER'S LOVER TO BRING IT BACK TO LIFE.

Below: ***Ambitious David Koresh had the looks of a rock star. When he failed to make the big time as a musician he set his sights on religion. After being thrown out of the Seventh Day Adventist Church, he swiftly worked his way up the ranks of the Branch Davidians until he was undisputed leader.***

Howell to breathe life back into it. In reply, Howell reported the grave-robbing escapade to the police. In order to prove his claim, Howell and his supporters embarked on a raid under the cover of darkness to snatch the body. George Rodin was equally determined he would not be exposed to the sheriff. There followed a shootout which ended in arrest for Howell and his friends. They were charged with attempted murder but never convicted. Instead, George Rodin found himself behind bars on a different charge.

The squabble between the two factions in 1987 ultimately spelled the start of absolute power for Howell in the Branch Davidians. He changed his name to David Koresh and ruled with an increasing brutality. With all charges against him dropped, the local lawmen had to return an arsenal of weapons they had seized during the troubles.

Koresh married a 14-year-old girl called Rachel Jones in Hollywood. She became mother to his son Cyrus and daughter Star.

How could a man hold so much sway over the lives of so many, for so long?

For a start, Koresh knew the workings of the Seventh Day Adventist Church well. He knew the emphasis laid on the content of the scriptures – and became an expert himself. It meant he was in a prime position to convert existing church members to his way of thinking.

Also, he knew church worshippers were told to expect the Second Coming at any

KORESH FORCED YOUNG GIRLS TO HAVE SEX WITH HIM – AND BEAT THEM VICIOUSLY AFTERWARDS.

Left: ***At meetings, disciples were bombarded for hours with the word according to Koresh. Koresh knew the Bible better than anyone else in the room – and he was clever enough to pervert the message to his own ends. For many his words had the ring of truth and they abandoned their loved ones and their homes to be with him at Waco.***

Below: ***It was known that Koresh had a stockpile of weapons at his Waco compound. After four men were killed in a shootout, the FBI was taking no chances. They moved heavyweight equipment like this M-1 tank into position during the 51-day siege. When the FBI got the go-ahead to move in, its men were fully protected. Bullets fired by the cultists bounced off the armoury.***

time. If he presented himself as that Second Coming, he knew he would win a core of dedicated followers.

To prepare the ground for manipulation, Koresh would cage his quarries in a marathon Bible class lasting for 10 hours or more. During that time he would rant endlessly about his beliefs, brooking no opposition from his audience. Here he could plant the seeds that would flourish into a dedicated belief.

There was also an element of fear which threaded through his teachings. He was, he insisted, the Keeper of the Seven Seals, and could trigger the end of the world. Those who accepted the word that he was the Lamb of God were warmly welcomed. There were kisses, hugs, flattery and a sense of belonging. Those who refuted the claims were cast out, insulted and frequently cursed.

Like all cult leaders, he found the easiest prey were people who had lost their jobs, were recently divorced or had suffered some other setback in their lives. They were looking for fulfilment and Koresh would pose as the answer to their prayers.

He spread his net worldwide, coming to Britain in 1988 to poach more supporters from the traditional Adventists. In advance of his visit came Steve Schneider, a trusted lieutenant who had once studied at Newbold College, the Adventists' centre near Bracknell, Berkshire.

The church turned down Schneider's request to use the church and college for a series of 'Bible meetings' featuring Koresh. Undeterred, he secured a house near the college campus which still lent it some established church authority. When Koresh arrived, he would hold meetings starting at 9 am and still in full swing after midnight. Weary and befuddled, his audience were massaged into his way of thinking.

Livingstone Fagan was there. He

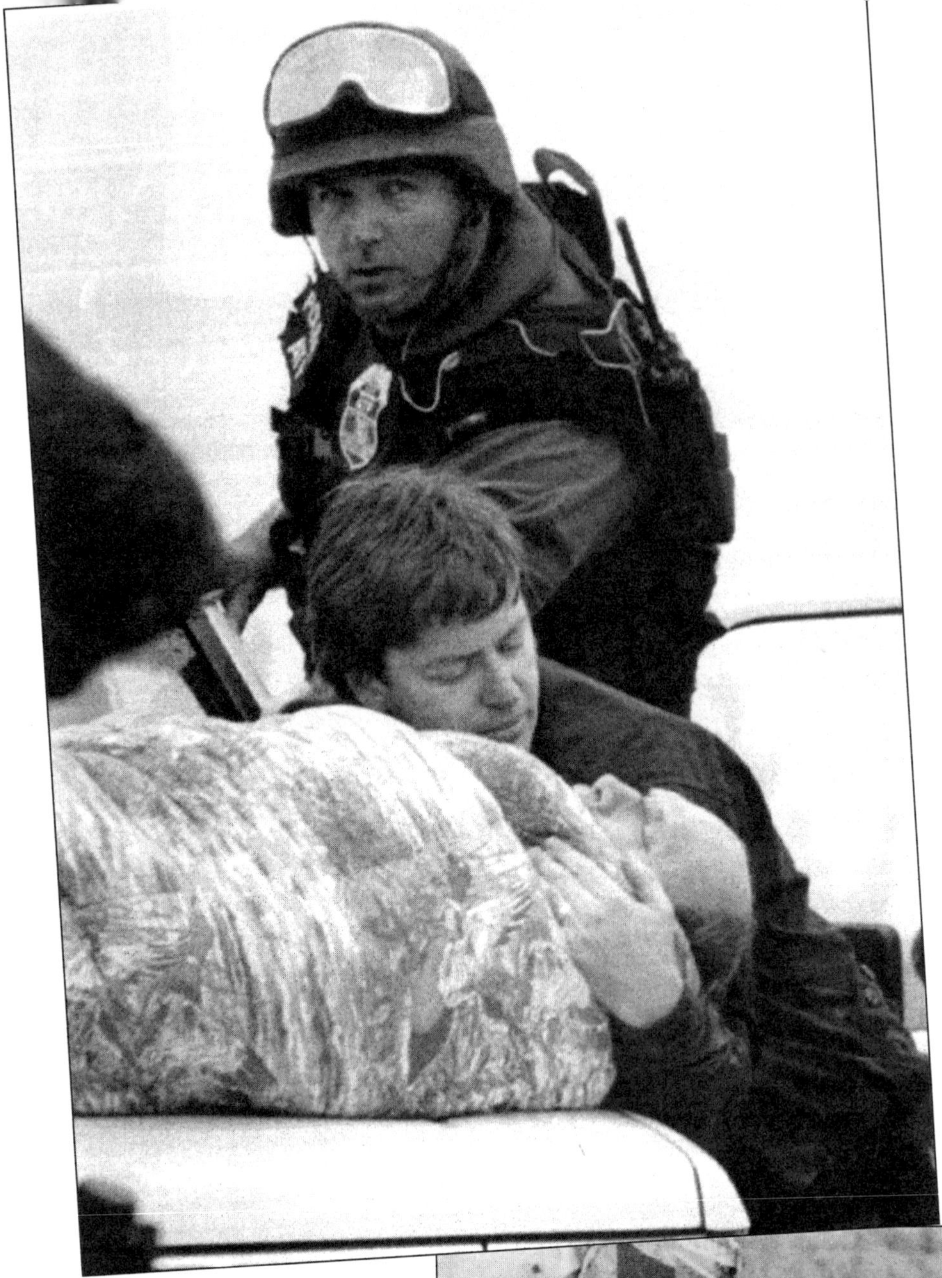

listened and readily believed all he heard about Koresh. Ordained as a pastor in the Seventh Day Adventist Church, he was defrocked after only three weeks after using his post to spread the word according to Koresh.

But he remained a firm believer and set about recruiting family and friends to the cause. The aim was to entice as many people as possible on a fact-finding mission to Waco to capture their imagination. In fact, many never returned home again. Once on Branch Davidian territory they were bombarded with the message morning noon and night. They were in turns humiliated and lauded by Koresh, who methodically worked away at destroying their egos and individuality.

From 5.30 am each day, the place was run like a military camp with extensive Bible study sessions. Koresh sought complete control, cutting his followers off from outsiders who would challenge his authority. At first, there was never any easy moment at which to leave. After a few weeks, most were too scared to up and go. They were told their name would go on a hit list and they would never be safe.

Australia and Hawaii were targeted as well by Koresh, greedy for increased power by boosting the size of his flock.

Above: ***A wounded agent is comforted on his way to hospital. In all 20 agents were injured in the raid.***

Right: ***ATF agents in full riot gear were determined to probe Koresh's spreading arsenal. But the cultists had been given a fair warning of their arrival. They were armed and ready when the agents appeared. The army of agents backed up by tanks did little to shake their determination to protect Koresh.***

Far right: ***Flags flew at half mast as investigators searched for the bodies of those who died.***

The clapboard farm was fortified and the number of arms on the property increased.

Meanwhile, Koresh was running amok inside. While men were told that celibacy was the road to heaven, women were seduced and enslaved by him. It was his Biblical destiny to sleep with 144,000 virgins, he preached.

But it didn't stop there. Soon he was indulging in three-in-a-bed romps and, worse, abusing young girls. In addition to sex, they faced beatings for imagined felonies. Koresh sired numerous children and bragged about his harem. No one questioned his right to rule. For protection he was surrounded by armed guards known as the 'mighty men'.

Worried families could only guess what was going on behind closed doors. On the face of it, the Koresh community appeared relaxed and contented. One British father, whose wife and 11-year-old daughter had joined Koresh, went to Waco to see for himself what was going on. He was impressed by the specially built play area and range of schooling facilities and returned reassured, saying: 'Everyone seemed normal to me. Everyone seemed happy.'

A DEATH PROPHECY

Among his teaching, Koresh prophesied he would appear on TV in 1993 – and then die by fire. But no one could guess at the truth of his vision until March of that year when the peace of everyday life at the compound was shattered forever.

There was deep concern at the number of weapons held at the enclave. Agents from the Bureau of Alcohol, Tobacco and

Above: ***Jean Holub during a news conference on 18 March. She had taped a message to Koresh, her grandson, pleading with him to end the siege of Mount Carmel peacefully.***

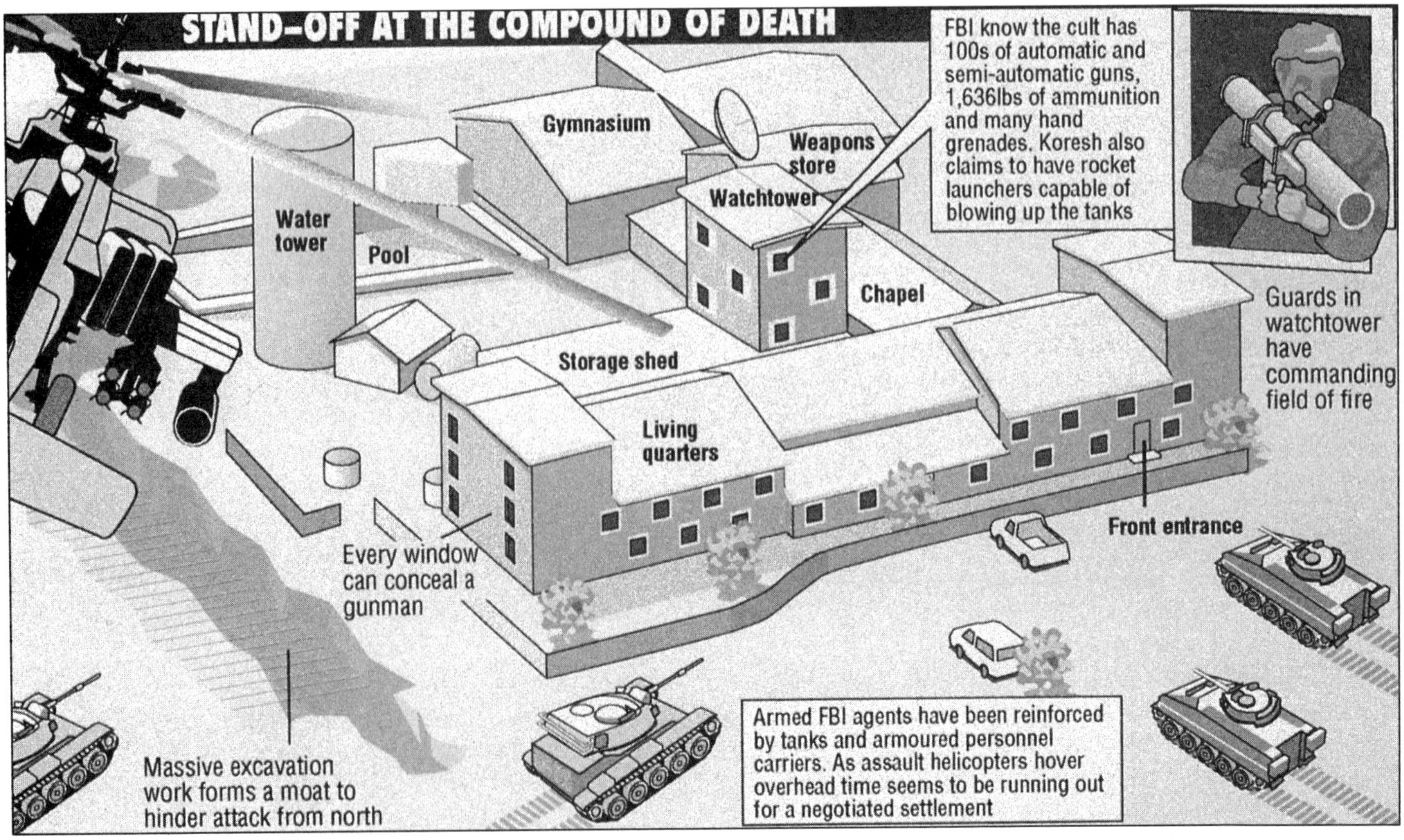

Above: ***A plan revealing how the FBI proposed an assault on Mount Carmel. Negotiators used high-tech gadgets to discover what was going on behind closed doors at the compound. Tiny cables could relay pictures of whole rooms while sophisticated bugging devices monitored even the most private conversation Koresh had.***

THE TRAUMATIZED CHILDREN ACTED LIKE ZOMBIES.

Right: ***Three of the surviving cultists on their way to a court hearing to face charges relating to the seige. Jaime Castillo, Derek Lovelock and David Thibodeau claimed the blaze was caused by heavy-handed government tactics. Koresh, they insisted, was on the verge of surrendering, ready to lead his people to safety.***

Firearms were determined that Koresh and his followers would be investigated.

An army of them, backed by tanks, circled the sect HQ and moved in to arrest Koresh. But as they advanced they were met with a volley of gunfire from an array of automatic weapons. There was even a blast from a 50 mm howitzer. Within seconds, 20 agents were hit, four of them fatally. In the ensuing gun battle, two sect members died: Briton Winston Blake and Koresh's own daughter, Star, aged 2.

The agents withdrew, dazed and bloodied but still determined to get their man. There was nothing for it but to sit and wait. It was the start of a 51-day siege. Negotiations followed deadlock. With enough food inside to last a year and sufficient arms to hold the agents at bay, it was clear Koresh was in no mood to cave in quickly.

While diplomats tried to coax and cajole Koresh from his lair, a more scientific approach was silently set in operation. Using an armoury of high-tech gadgets and bugs, the authorities were able to spy on cult members and their leader.

Fibre-optic cables like those used in hospital surgeries were placed in walls, air vents and chimneys and used to relay

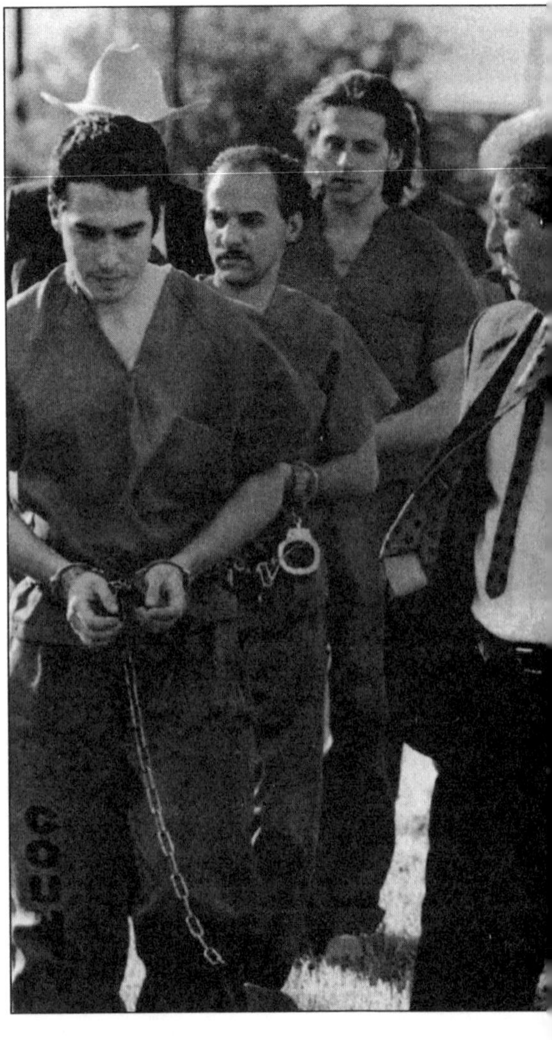

colour pictures of entire rooms. Aircraft flying overhead could monitor conversations inside and pinpoint people. Thermal imagers also helped to identify the whereabouts of those behind the walls.

As the days went past, agents began to draw a picture of life inside the compound – and learned Koresh had no plans to surrender.

In response to pleas, he did release a group of children. Shocked social workers caring for them afterwards declared they were like 'zombies'. They had been subject to the same indoctrination as their parents and now thought their adopted father had rejected them by casting them out. They were so deeply disturbed by their life-style and ordeal, they could barely communicate.

Finally, the Bureau decide charm diplomacy had run its course. It wanted Koresh and his crowd out of their hideaway – and quickly.

Koresh was talking more like a desperado than a saviour and by now the listening agents knew the extent to which he was abusing young children. They were unconvinced by promises from his lawyer that he would surrender his arms.

M-60 tanks trundled towards the compound firing harmless but disabling CS gas inside. The tanks would advance, shoot off some gas and then withdraw again to give those inside ample time to surrender. The only response was a blast of gunfire.

The disciples donned gas masks and retired to a prepared bunker at the heart of the complex. It was only when this last refuge was pierced by a tank that Koresh gave the order to die.

Agents insist fires were lit at three or more points around the site simultaneously after Koresh made his wishes known. Gunfire was also heard before agents penetrated the compound, giving rise to the theory that Koresh and his men shot those trying to escape.

Experts – who were concerned that tried and trusted methods to end the siege peaceably were ignored – have confirmed that Koresh would have probably chosen to die in a scorched earth sensation. It was unlikely he would have confided a mass suicide plan to anyone until moments before it occurred, they concur.

But the nine survivors are certain that there was no master plan for everyone to die, that David himself wanted to walk out alive and even that a date had been set for surrender.

It was a tank breaking into the compound knocking over a kerosene lamp that torched the place, not cult followers, they maintained. The tanks also collapsed inner stairways, leaving children trapped in a room upstairs.

The final truth may never be known. Few secrets were imparted from the badly charred remains of those who died. The only certainty is that an evil ruler of bodies and minds refused to die alone.

Above: ***Janet Reno had only become attorney general a matter of weeks before the Waco seige. After studying reports and analysis for a week, she sought permission from President Bill Clinton to move in on Mount Carmel and break the deadlock. She told him her concern was for the children inside at risk from poor sanitation and appalling disease.***

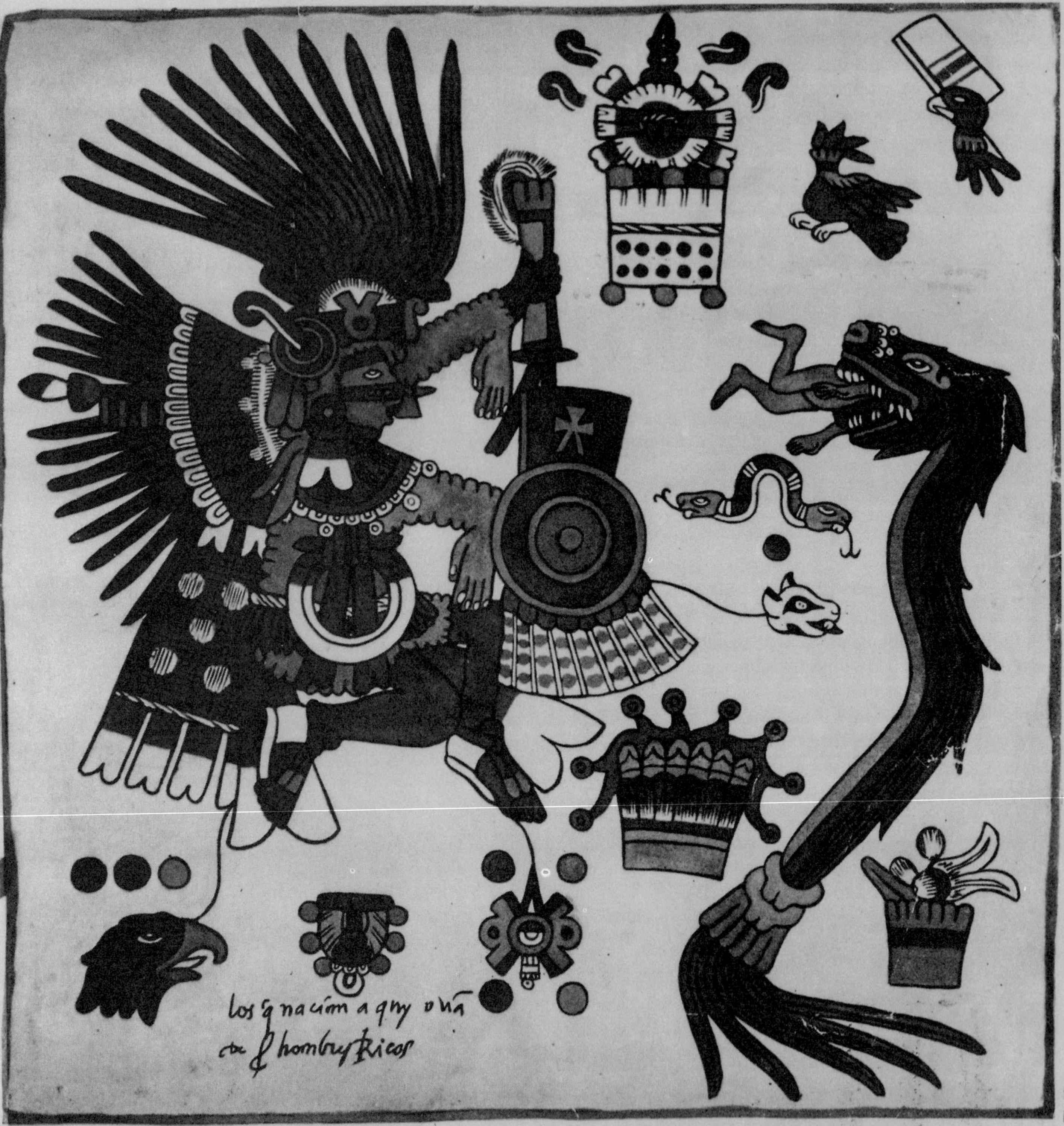

ANCIENT RITUALS

Bizarre, erotic, or simply cruel and bloodthirsty, the significance of many ancient rituals is shrouded in mystery. What is clear is that the ancient peoples never doubted that it was worth risking their lives for their strange beliefs.

A line of young men gathers on a remote, rocky beach. Ahead of them is a half-mile swim across waters teeming with sharks. Then a perilous race up a bare rock face, vying with their rivals for the best route.

Their goal? To be first to find a rare egg and return with it intact to their 'sponsor'.

It sounds like some weird and wonderful TV game show (with the man-eating sharks thrown in to boost ratings). In fact, this old religious ritual was regarded with enormous solemnity on Easter Island, that wild and craggy volcanic outcrop that has spawned one of the world's most mysterious civilizations.

The 'Bird Man' ritual was first noted in the 15th century, though its origins may date back much further. It is probably a unique ceremony and was devised to mark out great warriors who, for a year, would become the personal earthly envoys of the god Makemake. The seabird link stems from local legend – it was believed Makemake appeared on Earth in gull form.

So, in September of every year, the athletes would gather at the island's southern village of Orongo to make the hazardous swim across the straits to the island of Moto Nui.

Each contestant would be sponsored by a tribe warrior and the training and selection programme was worthy of any modern-day Olympic swimmer. But the contestants also had to be expert climbers capable of ascending the cliffs of Moto Nui at speed. Their task would then be to track down a nest of the Manutara (or Frigate) bird and bring back an egg to Easter Island.

Opposite: ***An Aztec eagle and serpent gods. Animals and birds had cherished places in Aztec culture and were credited with mystic powers – both good and evil. Eagles and seabirds were among the most revered.***

Below: ***These stone figures on Easter Island remain the subject of endless fascination for archaelogists. Were they simply sculptures or do the stones hold the secrets of some long-ago lost ritual?***

Above: ***The grand temple of ancient Mexico. Human sacrifice was a regular part of the Central American religions and this etching shows victims being hurled down the steps.***

The successful swimmer's sponsor would immediately be ordained Bird Man for the year and could look forward to a key role in many other important nature rituals.

It seems the Bird Man cult never really spread to other Polynesian islands, which worshipped their own deities. But its characteristics and themes are mirrored in dozens of other ancient rites around the globe.

Most seem to follow a similar thread: namely that the Nature gods, of whatever description, must be appeased to ensure sufficient food and guard against natural disasters such as drought or flooding. Often fertility ceremonies were interwoven, again to ensure productive farms and the birth of a new, healthy generation of future workers.

Where the rituals involved some kind of test, or act of courage, this helped reinforce the religion as a doctrine worth dying for.

A GAME OF SLAUGHTER

The Bird Men of Easter Island were therefore by no means unusual in harnessing athletic skills to religious ritual. In Central America Olmec priests invented a sport called 'The Ball Game', a cross between Spanish pelota, volleyball and soccer.

By 400 BC it was spreading to the Toltecs, Aztecs and Maya, who each adapted it to local rules.

Teams would play on H-shaped courts laid out north to south or east to west. A line was drawn between two high side walls and the aim was to nudge a large rubber ball into your opponent's half, using only hips, knees and elbows, under rules very close to volleyball.

A team could also score an outright victory by guiding the ball through either of a pair of stone rings which jutted out from each wall about 20 feet above the ground.

Such marksmanship was rare. The rings were only a little larger than the ball. But, bizarrely, if a player did succeed he was allowed to take the clothes and worldly goods of any spectators he and his team could catch.

It was not a poor man's pastime and in fact only noblemen were allowed to play. They kitted themselves out in protective padding, leather jerkins – even facemasks and gloves. Yet despite these safeguards serious injuries, even death, were accepted as part of the game.

Such intense action gave it a popular following, but it was the ritual significance that was the real hook.

The court was supposed to represent the

Universe. The stone rings were sunset and sunrise and the route of the ball portrayed the paths of the Sun and Moon.

Aztecs would study the course of a game intensely to see what it predicted for the future. In one case the Aztec ruler Montezuma played against a neighbouring chief to test the merit of a seer's claim that strangers would overthrow him.

Montezuma won the first few games but lost the match and, legend has it, it was not long afterwards that the assault on Mexico was started by Hernando Cortez.

The implications for teams which lost were immense. Their side bets could leave them so broke that they were forced into slavery to ensure they got food and board. The idea was that they could buy their freedom back for the same price if they ran into money.

For the Maya people the stakes were even higher. Some matches ended with the losing team ritually slaughtered.

If sport quickly became absorbed into ancient rites, dances and acting soon took on even more significance as a connecting link between mankind and Mother Nature.

FERTILITY RITES

Sometimes these took the form of a morale-boosting attempt to highlight people's mastery of the forces around them. One classic example of this is the bull-leaping dance of the Minoans, a culture which ruled Crete for 500 years from 1920 BC.

This dance required young men to somersault over a bull's horns, proving that man was indeed the dominant power on Earth. The animal, itself feted as an example of male fertility at its finest, was never harmed. Many historians believe the later Greek legend of the Minotaur is rooted in the bull-leaping ceremony.

The emphasis on man's dominance was, however, less common in rituals than the desire to appease the wild powers of

IF THEY LOST THE MATCH PLAYERS WERE IN DANGER OF LOSING THEIR FREEDOM – OR EVEN THEIR LIVES.

Below: ***The mythical Minotaur is one of many half-man-half-beast creatures that feature in the old religions. Here the Minotaur is about to be slain by the Greek, Theseus.***

Above: ***Pumpkins cut into the faces of monsters are a traditional part of Halloween today. The Celts called the festival Samain Eve. It was a night when the forces of magic poured from their boltholes in woods, caves and burial mounds.***

nature. Who wanted to spend time heralding the glory of humanity when the summer's harvest had just been wiped out by flooding?

In parts of Europe and Asia it is still the custom to build a straw figure, representing the Nature Spirit, which is then carried through the village accompanied by dozens of wailing, mourning women. Depending on local custom the straw man is then either buried, tossed into water (considered a useful rain charm) or brought back to life and carried among the rejoicing women back to the village.

Occasionally the straw doll is given a phallus – a plea to the fertility gods – and enclosed in a coffin.

Other forms of the ritual centre on dressing the doll in a man's shirt and carrying it to the boundary of a neighbouring village. Women then tear the figure to bits and hang its shirt on a sapling.

The tree is cut down soon afterwards and borne home amid much celebration. Folklore suggests it is the symbol of rebirth for humanity, which is itself portrayed in the form of the destroyed doll.

In some parts the effigy is replaced by a young man called the 'King of the May' (many nature rituals were and are performed around this month because it was an important pagan festival before Christianity) who is swathed in bark and bouquets of flowers.

At the end of the ceremony his attendants give him a head start before chasing after him. If he escapes them he holds office for a year. If they catch him he is subjected to a mock beheading, his crown is struck off and his 'corpse' carried on a bier to the nearest neighbouring village.

The idea behind this, seemingly, is to inflict the spirit of a useless king on the neighbours in the hope that it won't dog your own chances of future prosperity.

Other forms of nature worship include sword dancing or, more commonly in England, Morris dancing. Both are tributes intended to ensure that the seasons continue in their ordered manner, that the soil stays fertile and the crops arrive in abundance.

The Morris men and women, with their fussy white pleated shirts, white trousers or skirts with bells at the knee and hats covered with flowers, are still a common enough sight on English village greens.

Traditionally the leader bears a sword which has a piece of cake spiked on the point. As the dance progresses, slices are handed out to the audience who in turn are expected to cough-up some money to the 'Treasury', a money chest slung round the shoulders of a Morrisman called the Squire or Clown.

He will generally carry his symbol of office – a stick with a bladder tied to one end and a cow's tail at the other.

The dancers bear maces or wands, which they clash together during the course of the dance. Cups and lances also figure prominently and it is thought these are key symbols of what remains essentially a fertility rite steeped in mystery and legend.

Many old civilizations saved their reverence for the forces of nature – Sun and Moon, night and day, wind and sea and thunder and lightning. But sometimes tribal leaders have also found themselves elevated to the status of gods. This could mean their subjects regarded their well-being as crucial to the survival of the entire community.

It followed that if the leader got sick, the omen was bad. If he showed great courage, vigour or wisdom, the portents would be rosy.

This kind of adulation could, of course, cut both ways. There were established rules laid down to discover when a leader was past his best and needed replacing. If he stayed on, and wasn't up to the job, the god he represented could wreak a terrible revenge.

The methods used were both sneaky … and ruthless.

Earlier this century an old African tribe called the Shilluk, which lived close to the White Nile, would worship its king as a reincarnation of its legendary founder Nyakang. Nyakang was the rain-giver, on whom all life and prosperity depended. He had to be appeased at all costs.

A ROYAL EXECUTION

The problem for a king was that he could not be allowed to get old or decrepit. If he did, legend had it that men would die young, cattle would sicken and crops fail.

The tribe elders would therefore keep a close eye on their king as he advanced in years and one of the main tests of his health rested on how well he satisfied the sexual desires of his wives, of whom he had many.

If he failed to come up to their expectations they would report his performance to the chiefs who would then immediately condemn the king to death (there was no right of appeal in this court).

Often the first an unfortunate monarch would glean from such plottings would be on awakening from his mid-morning nap to find a long white cloth had been laid over his entire body. This indicated the grim news that sentence had been passed. The king would then be taken prisoner and starved to death, with a young maiden of the tribe assigned to tend his needs over his last days.

This method of execution was later abandoned as cruel after one, unknown, king suffered too long. It was replaced with a quicker – though equally horrific – end with the king strangled in a specially built execution hut.

A similar religious system existed in Nigeria until recent times. Here the Ju-Ju, or priest-king, was elected for seven years during which time he had the riches of his people heaped upon him. However, at the end of that time he was expected to kill himself, always assuming a usurper had not already succeeded in despatching him.

Despite the obvious drawbacks in running for priest-king it seems the exotic 7-year life-style attracted plenty of candidates who saw death afterwards as a price well worth paying.

In Ancient Britain the Celts had a similar system in which every king had his *geasa*, a nature spirit who ensured farming and prosperity would flourish. If crops failed or cattle died the king would take the rap for somehow displeasing his *geasa*. It is unclear whether he would suffer summary execution as a result.

The problem of choosing a new king was particularly tricky for the old religions.

IF THE KING FAILED TO SATISFY THE VORACIOUS SEXUAL APPETITES OF HIS MANY WIVES, HE PAID THE ULTIMATE PRICE.

Above: ***The Cerne Abbas giant. Childless women still sit on the tip of the figure's penis in the hope that it will help them conceive.***

CHILDLESS WOMEN RESORTED TO THE GIANT'S ENORMOUS PHALLUS IN A DESPERATE ATTEMPT TO CONCEIVE A CHILD.

Above: ***Julius Caesar saw the Druids as a dangerous and well-organized resistance movement. But he failed to stamp them out completely.***

Right: ***Druids worship at Stonehenge in 1974. Though many identify the religion with the monument, Stonehenge is at least 1,000 years older than the first Druids.***

A ruler might have had dozens of children, some born at almost the same time to different wives. Sorting out heirs was nigh on impossible and rather than hold an election Celtic Druid priests persuaded the people that they could identify the rightful heir by going into a 'bull dream' or trance.

This involved slaughtering a bull and allowing the chief Druid to gorge himself on the meat. He would then fall into a trance while others of his religion recited incantations over him.

Once the sated priest had recovered he would recount his dreams and deduce from them the identity of the new king.

THE OLD MAGIC

The Celts were particularly attached to ritual, to the point where it governed almost everything they did. It took on a supreme importance during the celebration of their two main seasons (warm and cold).

In Ireland all four main seasons were marked with festivals, the most important being Samain, a date we now call Halloween.

It marked the end of one year and the beginning of another and was a time when cattle would be herded in and slaughtered for winter meat supplies. Only those beasts needed for breeding would be spared.

Samain Eve was also the night when the world was deemed to be assaulted by the forces of magic pouring from old caves and burial mounds. It was thought that mortals could pass the other way into the kingdoms of fairies and hobgoblins.

Folk legends linked to Samain refer to the god Dagda, always portrayed as a figure of immense strength and appetite and carrying a mighty club. He was considered a god of fertility, rejuvenation and endurance and among the many Celtic tributes to him is the massive chalk-cut figure in Dorset – the Cerne Abbas giant – whose most striking features are an enormous phallus and serrated club.

To this day childless women sometimes sit on the tip of the figure's penis in the hope mystical forces will help them to conceive.

The other main Celtic festival, Beltane, was celebrated at the beginning of May. It was a time when cattle could be driven back to graze on open grassland and was marked by the burning of beacons across the land.

Often terrified animals would be driven between two blazing bonfires, a rite thought to protect them from disease.

Perhaps more than any other ancient British Isles religion, the Druids are remembered as a people who made human

sacrifice a way of life. The most usual method would be by knife, spear or sword, with the blood of the chosen one poured on to sacred objects such as stones or old trees. But there are also recorded instances of burnings, drownings and hangings.

Caesar described in his writings how Gaulish Celts would build massive wicker baskets, pack them with living victims (preferably, though not necessarily criminals) and set the frame alight. This sacrifice was supposed to ensure the well-being of the tribe.

Drownings would be performed under strict ceremonial rules, the hapless victim forced headfirst into a barrel of water and held under until all struggling ceased.

Life may have seemed cheap, but to the Celts death was never considered an end. So obsessed were Celtish warriors with the fate of their victims that they would decapitate them and suspend a gruesome array of trophies on the bridles of their horses. The aim, it appears, was to bring the ghosts of the vanquished under the power of the victor.

For years Stonehenge, one of the world's greatest prehistoric sites, was thought to be a temple for Druidic rites. Some evidence has been advanced suggesting that the Druids did, at one time, use it for their rituals.

But in fact Stonehenge is at least 1,000 years older than the Druid religion, built with surprising skill by the ancient Britons as either a temple or some kind of astronomical observatory.

Many elaborate theories have been advanced as to its true purpose but none have produced solid proof.

Above: ***Stonehenge. Anyone who has visited the strange forbidding stones can only marvel at the atmosphere they generate. The reason for the construction is still questionable – was it a site for ritual ceremony or some giant astronomical computer?***

THE EGYPTIAN WAY OF DEATH

If Stonehenge was a wonder of ancient architecture, the great pyramids of Egypt are close to a miracle. Their purpose as burial chambers is clear, but the extraordinarily precise design, and elaborate death rituals, gives glimpses of an intelligence and civilization which modern people still find difficult to fathom.

The kings of Ancient Egypt were considered to need to have all their worldly goods entombed with them when they died. Food, weapons, clothes, money and jewels were seen as necessities of death upon which the fragile new spirit would rely as he or she wandered through the afterlife.

This was also why the Egyptians developed the art of mummification, or embalming, a ritual elevated almost to an art form in its aim to preserve the body for the convenience of the soul.

First, all internal organs would be carefully removed from the corpse (on the grounds that they would decay quickest). Then the body would be dried out with salt water, dusted with a type of bicarbonate of soda, wrapped in bandages, soaked in oils and finally placed in a painted coffin.

Throughout the rite, magical spells

would be chanted to ensure the spirit could look forward to everlasting life in the underworld.

Some of the richest Egyptians would even set up a trust fund to pay a priest's salary after their death.

His main job would be to replenish the grave regularly with food and water, removing the rotting morsels left on previous visits.

In recent years followers of the so-called pyramidology cult – founded by those who believe that mystical forces flow through the pyramids – have used these customs to construct their own incredible theories.

Some claim that a tomato placed under a precisely constructed and sited pyramid model will take longer to rot than one left next to it in an ordinary cardboard box. The same strange forces are said to sharpen razor blades mysteriously.

No conclusive scientific proof has ever been produced to support this claim.

Whatever their hidden qualities, the pyramids were marvels of early

Above: ***Embalmers at work on the body of a wealthy Egyptian. All internal organs would have been removed in a process interwoven with magical rites.***

Right: ***The Cheops pyramid and the Sphinx. The pyramid contains around 6 million tons of stonework covering an area of 15 acres. It is the only one of the original seven wonders of the ancient world still surviving.***

engineering. One, the tomb of the King-God Cheops, is the only one of the original seven wonders of the ancient world still surviving.

Like most pyramids it was the focal point of a meticulously constructed complex of funeral buildings, all designed under strict ritualistic rules to safeguard the royal journey into the spirit world.

The pyramid of Cheops covers 15 acres, is 450 feet tall and contains an estimated six million tons of stonework. At least two 'emergency' tombs were crafted in case the king died suddenly before the masterpiece was complete.

The actual tomb chamber, measuring 16 feet by 34 feet, was positioned high above ground level. The king's stone coffin was laid on a tiled floor and on the face of the mummy was laid a gold mask dripping with jewels. Around it were arranged the inevitable weaponry and vitals, and even Cheops's favourite furniture found its way inside.

As the death rite ended the coffin, and all exits from the chamber, were sealed. On their way out labourers pulled away the props that held up three massive blocks. These slid over the burial chamber entrance with such precision that it was impossible to tell from outside where the door lay.

When Cheops's grave was eventually raided in the 9th century by the Caliph al-Mamum, he could find no way in and was reduced to boring straight through the stone itself.

Even the narrow ascending passage used by priests as an escape tunnel after administering last prayers was plugged by huge pieces of granite.

Just for good measure word was spread that terrible curses had been laid ready to descend upon the head of anyone who dared to attempt a break-in.

Around the pyramid lay many monuments and the funeral temple where priests carried out the 'survival rites' which it was hoped would ensure the king's safe transit to the other world. Excavations in nearby rock have uncovered small boats, though their purpose has never been explained.

THE UNIQUE POWERS OF THE PYRAMIDS ARE STILL UNDER INVESTIGATION TODAY.

Below: ***A model boat from the Tutankhamun exhibition at the British Museum. The Egyptians believed their kings would need all worldly goods with them in their tombs for use in paradise.***

THEY MADE THEIR ENEMIES' SKULLS INTO DRINKING GOBLETS AND DELIGHTED IN DRINKING WINE FROM THEM.

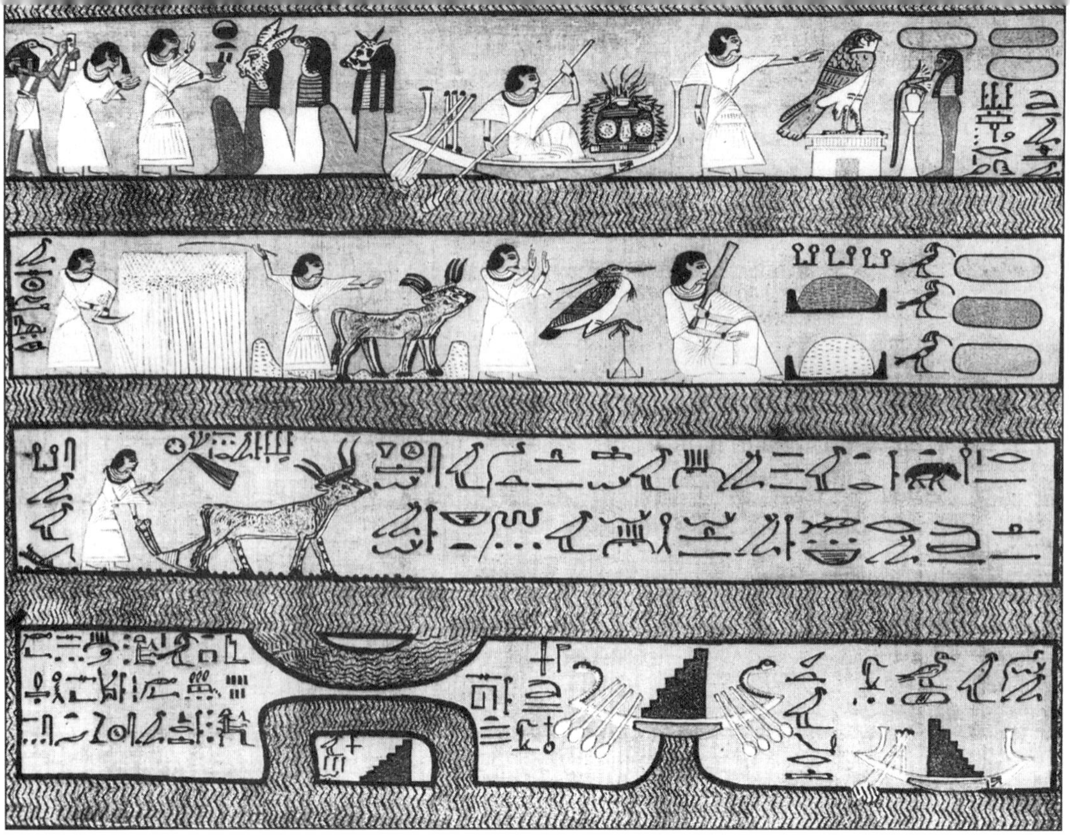

Right: *Papyrus from the Ancient Egyptians' 'Book of the Dead' shows departed souls in their lives on the 'other side'.*

Below: *Tutankhamun's gold death mask. No wonder the tomb robbers of ancient Egypt risked their lives to plunder the world's wealthiest tombs.*

RITUAL ATROCITIES

If death rituals were important to the Egyptians, they were a way of life to the Scythians, perhaps the single most powerful tribe ever to roam the Steppelands of Russia.

Almost every important occurrence would be marked by ritual atrocities and even the simple act of having guests to dinner was bound by long-established ground rules.

It was the custom to make drinking goblets out of the skulls of enemies and any visitor sipping his wine from one would be regaled with colourful – and rather too detailed – accounts of the passing of its original owner.

Warriors were expected to drink the blood of the first opponent they killed, a ritual linked to enslaving the fallen man's ghost. And once a year Scythian fighters would gather for a festival to drink from skull cups and tot up the number of slayings each had achieved over the previous 12 months.

Any warrior whose tally was nil was treated with contempt by his brothers and forced to endure incessant jeering and teasing at the hands of the women and children.

For the Scythian kings who reigned 2,000 years ago, the expectation of a glorious afterlife was a view cherished from early childhood.

And when the grim reaper called on them he could count on a great many more souls into the bargain.

It was accepted that a king would need his loyal servants in death just as much as in life. If he died, they would have to die too.

According to the 5th-century Greek historian Herodotus, the death rituals of the Scythians – centred on tombs called *kurgans* – were among the most elaborate and complicated ever devised.

He wrote: 'When a king dies they dig a great square pit and, when it is ready, they take up the corpse which has been previously prepared in the following manner.

'The belly is slit open, cleaned out, and filled with aromatic substances, crushed galingale [a sweet-smelling plant] parsley seed and anise. It is then sewn up once more and the whole body coated with wax.

'The corpse is laid in the tomb on a mattress with spears fixed in the ground on either side to support a roof of brush laid on wooden poles. In other parts of the great square pit various members of the king's household are buried beside him: one of his concubines, his butler, cook, groom, steward and chamberlain – all of them strangled.

'Horses are buried too – and gold cups – and a selection of his other treasures.

'This ceremony over, everybody with great enthusiasm sets about raising a mound of earth, each competing with his neighbour to make it as big as possible. At the end of a year another ceremony takes place: they take 50 of the best of the king's remaining servants, strangle and gut them, stuff the bodies with chaff and sew them up again.

'These servants are native Scythians, for the king has bought no slaves, but chooses people to serve him from amongst his subjects.'

Some 2,000 years later it is easy to dismiss the Scythians and Druids as bloodthirsty heathens meting out pointless deaths.

Yet it seems they had none of the doubts of the modern age as to the promise of an afterlife. To them, rituals were the link to an unknown world – visible evidence of the life cycle.

Bizarre and brutal … but never pointless.

Above: ***These scenes from Scythian life were found on 3rd- or 4th-century vases found north of the Black Sea. Scythian kings would often take their entire household with them to the grave. They reasoned that they would need servants just as much in death as in life.***

SHIPWRECKS
Riches of the sea

Billions of pounds' worth of treasure lies abandoned in wrecked ships, waiting to be snatched from the clutch of the jealous sea. For those daredevils prepared to risk their lives the rewards are obvious: a fortune in gold and silver, or an agonizing death.

There are few places in the world that can match the Isles of Scilly's record for disaster at sea. For centuries mariners on the Western Approaches to England learned the hard way how this ten-square-mile stretch of treacherous rocks and reefs could destroy any ship whose master was foolish enough to stray too close.

Many thousands lost their lives through poor navigation or were dragged to their deaths in lethal currents amid some fierce Atlantic storm. Not for nothing is one stretch of this unforgiving coast called 'Hell Bay'.

The Scillies are truly a ships' graveyard and in these shallow waters beneath ever-shifting sands hoards of treasure still lie untouched. So far the islands have produced two outstanding successes for the marine archeologists.

The first was the wreck of the *Colossus*, the second that of HMS *Association*. Both finds owed much to the bravery and skill of the late Cornishman Roland Morris, a man who fashioned the art of modern-day treasure-hunting.

For as long as he could remember the story of the *Association* had fascinated Morris. The events of the wild night she went down with the pride of her fleet

Opposite: ***Admiral Sir Clowdisley Shovell. Hours before the HMS* Association *disaster he had feared his fleet was off course. Yet a conference among his captains did little to improve matters. The navigational position of the ships was estimated too far south and in the dead of night they blundered onto a lethal Scilly reef.***

Below: ***The* Association *and other ships on the rocks – 1,648 lives were lost that night and the sea around Scilly heaved with the bodies of young men.***

Above: ***Islanders find the body of Sir Clowdisley washed up on beach. They buried him just above the high-water mark at Porth Hellick, St Mary's Island. The body was later recovered and given a full state funeral at Westminster Abbey.***

THE BRITISH FLEET SAILED PROUDLY ONWARDS, MERE HOURS FROM HOME – AND DISASTER; BEFORE DAWN THE SEA WOULD HEAVE WITH CORPSES.

remain probably the greatest Royal Navy loss in home waters. It was a night the waters around Scilly heaved with the corpses of young men.

AN ERROR OF JUDGEMENT

The 90-gun *Association* was the flagship of Admiral of the White Sir Clowdisley Shovell, one of the most experienced seamen of his day. On 29 September 1707 he set sail from Gibraltar after taking part in the siege of Toulon. English sea power was at its height and Sir Clowdisley's men o' war, which totalled 12 ships of the line, would have been an awe-inspiring sight as they headed for home waters.

The vessels included the 100-gun *Royal Anne*, flagship of Sir George Byng (Vice-Admiral of the Blue), the 96-gun *St George*, captained by James Lord Dursley, the 70-gun *Eagle*, under Captain Robert Hancock, and the 48-gun *Romney* under Captain William Coney. There were also four fireships, among them HMS *Firebrand* and her master Captain Francis Piercy.

On the morning of Wednesday 22 October the fleet was approaching the mouth of the English Channel. Sir Clowdisley ordered three vessels to be detached from the main body to Falmouth, enabling advance preparations to be made for the reception of the entire fleet. Around midday *Lennox*, *Valeur* and *Phoenix* steered ahead on an easterly course. By nightfall it was clear they had fallen victim to a serious navigational error.

All three ships fell among the Scilly rocks and it was only the skill of the captains which prevented serious loss of life. *Lennox* and *Valeur* managed to keep clear and later anchored off the main island, St Mary's, but *Phoenix* was holed and had to be beached close to the island of Tresco to stop her sinking. The repairs later forced her to convert to a sixth-rate warship.

Back at the main fleet Sir Clowdisley was himself in trouble. He now suspected he was off-course and ordered his ships to heave to while soundings were taken. There followed a brief counsel of all the sailing masters and a consensus was reached. They were almost certainly around the latitude of Ushant, it was agreed, which meant a due easterly course would take them safely into the open waters of the English Channel.

Only one master dissented – Captain

Henry Hobart of the *Panther*. He argued strongly that they were much closer to the Scillies than was being suggested and risked being blown on to some of the outlying reefs. It was a brave speech, and his estimated position was, in fact, extremely close to the mark. But Sir Clowdisley overruled him and ordered the fleet to steer due east.

Why the seamanship of him and most of his captains was so sadly lacking will always be a mystery. Perhaps it was an eagerness to get home, over-confidence in their instincts or simply a blind determination not to lose an argument. Whatever the reason, they were now only hours from disaster.

By 6 pm the ships were underway again and the die leading them to certain doom was cast. As the fleet edged forward Hobart had a growing sense of dread. He could not ignore his admiral but he had a duty to save the lives of his crew if possible. Quietly, almost without being noticed, the *Panther* glided slowly down to the southern flank of the fleet where she remained one of the few ships which didn't have to change course.

THE WRATH OF THE SCILLIES

By now the weather was muggy and stormy and the watch on HMS *Association* – the ship leading the vanguard – was having understandable difficulty spying through the gloom. At around 8 pm she struck on the deadly Gilstone reef and sank with all hands. *Eagle* and *Romney* quickly followed her to their doom and *St George* also ran on, only to be lifted off minutes later by a gigantic wave.

Firebrand was lost, though 25 of her crew were saved, but the most remarkable escape was engineered by the *Royal Anne*, whose officers thought fast enough to set the topsails and weather the storm only a few yards away from the teeth of more rocks.

When Navy men later checked the muster lists for the wrecked ships the appalling carnage was finally laid bare. At least 1,648 lives were lost in the space of a few hours, among them Sir Clowdisley's. His body floated ashore at Porth Hellick, a sheltered cove on St Mary's, and the local folk buried him just above the high tide mark. According to one (unlikely) legend he was still alive on the beach but was murdered by an old crone hunting booty from the wrecks who had spotted his expensive rings. It is said the woman confessed on her deathbed, but no record was ever kept of her name.

Sir Clowdisley's body was later recovered by the Navy and taken to Plymouth aboard the *Salisbury*. From there it was brought to Westminster Abbey for a state funeral with full military honours.

Three years later the first treasure-hunters had moved on to the site of the *Association* wreck, though it seems with only limited success. A letter to the *London Letter*, an old Scottish newspaper, of 9 July 1710 read: 'We hear from Scilly that the gentlemen concerned in the wreck where Sir Clowdisley Shovell was cast away have taken several iron guns and seven brass guns, with a cable, and have found the *Association* in four fathom at low water, the hull of the ship being whole, wherein there is a vast treasure – the Queen's Plate, several chests of money, beside ten chests of Sir Clowdisley's own, with great riches of the Grandees of Spain. 'The divers go down

HOBART'S SENSE OF IMPENDING DOOM GREW STRONGER AS HE TRIED TO EDGE HIS SHIP INTO A SAFER POSITION.

Below: ***Lady Hamilton, mistress of Lord Nelson and wife of Sir William Hamilton. At least Sir William managed to come to terms with her infidelity. He never quite got over the loss of his priceless cargo.***

Above: ***Turner's*** **St Michael's Mount.** ***Scenes such as this fire dreams of long-lost treasure in every amateur scuba diver.***

in a copper engine and continue two hours under water.'

But the report goes on to hint that high winds and 'boisterous' seas had already scattered much of the sunken hoard. A fortune in pieces of eight and pieces of four still lay waiting to be found.

Some 91 years after the *Association* foundered it was the turn of HMS *Colossus* to suffer the wrath of the Scillies. She was another of the Navy's front-line ships, a 74-gun man o' war of about 1,700 tons.

At least her skipper, George Murray, could hardly be blamed for losing her. He'd hove to just off St Mary's and, seeing the signs of a vicious Atlantic storm brewing, secured her with three cables. Within minutes of the full fury of the storm sweeping in, one cable had parted and two others dragged. At dark she was on the rocks and her priceless cargo, a collection of ancient vases from the Mediterranean, was lost.

The vases – more than 1,000 of them – belonged to Sir William Hamilton (whose wife Emma was Nelson's mistress), and had been amassed during his time as British government minister in charge of Sicily. That terrible night he also lost large marble friezes, terracotta, bronzes and some fabulous Greek and Italian jewellery.

It would have been limited consolation to him to learn that most of the crew saved themselves in the rigging and only one man, quartermaster Richard King, died.

TREASURE TROVE

So it was that the fate of these ships would become intertwined, thanks to the tenacity of Roland Morris. He'd studied their history for most of his life and knew the waters well. During the war he'd worked tirelessly off the Cornish coast as a salvage

Right: ***Turner's*** **The Shipwreck.** ***This would have been a tragically familiar scene to seamen of the 18th and 19th centuries.***

THE TREASURE-HUNTER WAS DETERMINED TO COMMIT MARINE SUICIDE IN A HOME-MADE DIVING BELL.

Left: *Faulkner's* **The Shipwreck,** *1827. The sight of any vessel on the rocks was enough to bring locals running to the nearest shoreline in their scores, in search of wrecked cargo.*

diver, building up a massive personal dossier on the most likely locations of known wrecks. But it wasn't until 1967 that he was able to put that knowledge to the test.

Throughout the early sixties interest had been growing in the fate of Sir Clowdisley's fleet. However, confusing marks and entries on old maps meant the precise location was far from certain.

Between 1965 and 1967 the Naval Air Command Sub Aqua Club used inshore minesweepers manned by the Royal Navy Reserve to search for the *Association*. They found it right at the end of their allotted time, on 4 July 1967, resting in sand beneath the Gilstone Ledge.

It was left to Morris to confirm what the team suspected. He'd obtained a salvage licence from the Ministry of Defence for the *Association* and had already guessed, from his knowledge of currents and seabed movements, that she lay on the Gilstone. Within days of his operation commencing he'd located three bronze cannons and Sir Clowdisley's personal plate.

At first Morris used explosives to free the cannon but was forced to stop amid furious objections from the National Maritime Museum and the Institute of Archaeology. Eventually sheer persistence was rewarded and the team recovered a huge cache of coins, including Spanish pieces of eight, silver crowns and golden guineas and Portuguese 4,000 *reis* pieces.

The find sparked the marine equivalent of the Californian gold rush as dozens of unauthorized treasure-hunters converged on the spot. In the excitement two of the enthusiastic amateur boats capsized and one die-hard fortune seeker even attempted to launch himself on the *Association* in a copper diving-bell he'd made himself. Fortunately, Morris was able to talk him round.

Eight years later, armed with a British government licence, Morris achieved his second major triumph. He led a four-man team onto the ship he believed to be the *Colossus* and quickly gained confirmation in the form of a Greek potsherd. The treasure trove that followed set the world of marine archeology alight.

The team divided its seabed search area

Below: *1829 shipwreck engraving. Treasure ships such as this could scatter cargo for miles. The combination of shifting sands and unpredictable currents made the treasure-hunter's task enormously difficult.*

Above: ***Scenes of panic aboard the wreck of the* Deutschland, *1875. Survivors scramble to reach the safety of a tug.***

Below: ***Wrecked and saved. How the* Boy's Own Paper *depicted the drama of a shipwreck.***

into square metres with a man assigned to search each square four times. By the end of the salvage operation they had brought up more than 7,400 fragments dating back to the 4th century. Handles, rims, bases, bowls and cups were painstakingly logged and reassembled under the watchful eye of the British Museum.

After the *Colossus*, Morris entered semi-retirement, concentrating his energies on his Penzance restaurant, the Admiral Benbow. He would later take his greatest secret to his grave.

A GRISLY END

If Roland Morris drew on instinct and perseverance for results, Herbo Humphreys is the man who has turned the art of treasure-hunting into a science.

His hunting ground is the eastern Atlantic – especially the Little Bahama Bank – a sea area where many a Spanish merchantman met a grisly end. Just as the *Association* and *Colossus* fascinated and tantalized Morris, so the 'Floating Fort Knox', that is the *Maravillas*, has been an abiding challenge for Humphreys.

The *Maravillas* lies on Little Bahama, her fabulous cargo spread over a massive debris field. Her official manifest shows that around £600 million (at today's prices) of bullion, coins and jewels went down with her. However, historians estimate she could have had up to 11 times as much in contraband aboard. They believe around 90 chests of gold and silver lie somewhere on the seabed.

Humphreys, a former pilot, ship's captain, parachutist and Vietnam veteran, had only two interests as a boy – boats and business. He made his fortune in his teens,

Left: ***A picture that sums up the romance, drama and danger of a storm at sea in 1896. It shows Captain Nutman of the wrecked vessel* Aidar *refusing to leave an injured crewman as a lifeboat approaches.***

staking the £5,500 he won in a horse-riding competition on Philippines Gold at 25 cents a share. He later sold the stock at $30.

From there it was a tour of Vietnam, a property and travel business and a hotel investment on the Cayman Islands. An avowed anti-communist, he worked through peaceful means to undermine the Sandanistas in Nicaragua and later took the crusade against extremism on to Guatemala, Laos and the Philippines.

Below: ***Wreck of the* Cromdale, *1913. She broke up inside two hours during a ferocious south-westerly storm in British waters.***

Above: ***The* Campania *sinking after a collision in 1918 with HMS* Revenge. Campania *had been converted into one of the world's first aircraft carriers.***

Below: ***A pair of schooners on the rocks in Bigbury Bay, south Devon, England, in 1925.***

On the way he logged the possible sites of a lot of interesting shipwrecks. When the communist threat died down, and with his business empire in sound shape, he began to devote more time to his hobby of finding sunken treasure. More especially, finding the *Maravillas*.

The ship – full title *Nuestra Señora de las Maravillas* – was heading home to Cadiz, in Spain, from Havana when disaster struck. On the night of 4 January 1656 her crow's nest watch had clearly been in a mellow and relaxed mood amid the beautifully calm seas, but his mood changed in an instant when he spotted white water churning almost underneath the ship's bows.

The *Maravillas* had somehow drifted on to Little Bahama's western edge … and the rest of her fleet were close behind. The captain ordered cannon fire to warn the other masters away, but it was too late. His vessel was rammed by another ship and began to founder.

As she went down many of the 650 people aboard pleaded with priests such as Don Diego Portichelo de Ribadenevra, of the Holy Metropolitan Church, Lima, for absolution. In a colourful and emotional account of the mayhem, he later told a Spanish marine investigation at Castile: 'The confusion of the people was so great that they did not realize the importance of the sails to get them out of danger and instead occupied themselves in trying to stem the flow of the water pouring into the ship.

'With the sails idle, the currents rapidly drove the ships towards the banks. She bumped against the rocks so forcefully that her seams began to crack. Though the people were bailing with four pumps and pails the water rose as high as the second deck.

Above: *A floating coffin. The wreck of the* **Morro Castle** *attracted huge crowds of sightseers at Asbury Park, New Jersey, on 9 September 1934.*

'Up to that time I had heard confessions from many people, among them Admiral Don Matias de Orellana who told me that we would surely die and that I should grant absolution to everyone … they took me to the poop deck with many people following us who wanted to confess. They told me I should confess them in general and that they did not want to die without it. Noticing their determination and given the short time that remained for us I wasted no words and abbreviated as much as possible.'

All around him men were diving into the seas to find certain death. With their pockets still crammed with gold they sank to the bottom like stones. Portichelo de Ribadenevra told the inquiry how he prepared to swim for it, tearing off his shirt to reduce his weight in the water. He said: 'There I was, left in my underwear, the crucifix that I had brought with me in my hand.

'At that time I heard a voice saying "Is there some priest who can absolve me for I have been the greatest sinner in the world?" I stood up on the hatch cover with some difficulty. My companions held me by the belt of my underpants. I don't know how, I suddenly found myself forgetting about the danger I was in. I raised my voice and told them: "Here is a priest. Say now: I sinned, my Lord God, and I shall absolve you."'

So it carried on through that grim night. Some two score souls survived clinging to the wreckage but more than 600 were doomed. By the time dawn arrived and another ship of the fleet came to their rescue all that could be heard was the sound of a quiet hymn floating across the water on the breeze.

The passage of the years has not lessened the scale of the tragedy. However, it has ensured that nothing about Humphreys's task is easy. Neither is it cheap.

The payroll includes marine archivists in Spain, restorers and marketing experts to turn artefacts raised into hard cash and the staggering £180,000 per month cost of operating on the 160-mile patch of seabed for which the Bahamian Government has granted salvage rights.

Humphreys has brought in the most advanced gear in the world, such as satellite-linked global navigation aids, able to pinpoint the user on the Earth's surface to 200 yards, sonar, magnometers and a highly skilled crew of divers and engineers. He has ploughed £3 million of his personal wealth into the project and has so far pulled out about the same in finds. But with up to

THE MEN JUMPED OVERBOARD BUT THE STOLEN GOLD IN THEIR POCKETS SENT THEM PLUMMETTING TO THE BOTTOM OF THE OCEAN.

Above: ***English fire-ships amongst the Spanish Armada. The Armada vessels, wrecked in 1588, are the richest known to be lying on the ocean bed.***

70 outside investors wanting a slice of the action, the pressure to find the *Maravillas*'s treasures never lets up.

THE RICHEST WRECKS

Herbo, of course, is not the only treasure-hunter in the game. And because there are so many rich wrecks around the globe there's plenty of room for others to play … provided they have the cash.

Listing the richest wrecks of the seas is an impossible task. However, the 12 that follow all figure high in every treasure-hunter's dreams.

The Spanish Armada: sunk in 1588 at various locations between France and Iceland, but mostly concentrated around south-west Ireland and the Hebrides. The ships' cargoes of gold ducats, jewel-studded artefacts and personal jewellery is, literally, priceless.

The *Flor de la Mar*: this Portuguese vessel foundered in 1512 off the Straits of Malacca between Indonesia and Malaya, close to Diamond Point. She carried diamonds, rubies, Chinese and Arabic coins and gold and bejewelled statues of animals. Some historians estimate the value at an incredible £5.5 billion, and not surprisingly Portugal, Indonesia and Malaysia have all claimed a share if and when the wrecked booty is ever raised. Until then, the seas around are regularly patrolled by gunboats.

Sixteen unidentified Spanish galleons: they were part of a 20-strong fleet wrecked en route from Veracruz to Spain in 1553. The hulls are thought to lie off Padre Island, Texas, and the estimated value of the gold and silver bullion aboard is put at £1.2 billion.

The Mendoza fleet: Spanish ships sunk in 1614 somewhere off Cape Catoche, Yucatan. Treasure is valued at around £600 million. Mystery surrounds the fate of this fleet, commanded by Admiral Juan de la Cueva y Mendoza, which simply vanished during passage between Mexico and Cuba.

La Madelena: another Spanish ship, which went down off Cape Canaveral, Florida, in 1563. She carried more than 50 tons of silver ingots, a ton of gold, jewellery and 1.25 million *pesos*. The victim of a hurricane, only 16 of her 300 passengers and crew survived.

The *SS Merida*: an American ship, she was carrying £350 million worth of Mexican gold ingots when she collided with a steamship while sailing from Veracruz to New York. The wreck site, off Virginia Capes, is known but in 1933 an attempt to recover the gold failed.

The *Santissima Trinidad*: sunk in 1711, 15 miles west of Havana, she carried assorted treasure today worth about £300 million. Unlike her four sister ships, which were also lost in a ferocious storm, her remains have never been traced. Ironically, hers was by far the richest manifest.

Jamaican Merchant: a pirate ship which had enjoyed rich pickings off the Haitian coast. She is believed to have gone down east of the Ile de Vache together with her £270 million booty.

The *John Barry*: an American vessel lost off Oman on 28 August 1944. She carried 1,800 tons of silver worth a conservative £142 million.

La Lutine: one of the most famous wrecks in the world, her bell still hangs in the Lloyd's of London marine insurance house. Traditionally it is rung once for bad news, twice for good. Most of the *Lutine*, however, still lies beneath the waves of Terschelling Island in the Zuider Zee, Holland. Originally a French frigate, she was captured by the British and was being used to deliver pay to a British garrison at Texel Island before sailing on to Hamburg to deliver £130 million worth of gold and silver bars to German merchants. Her bullion is now protected by some of the deadliest fast currents in the world.

Rommel's treasure: this was reputed to have been cast overboard in strongboxes in the Gulf of Bastia, east Corsica. The treasure included gems, art treasures and precious stones looted by the Germans and worth around £80 million. The six chests were cast away on 18 September 1943 to keep them from the Allies. They have never been seen since.

Above: ***Wreck in Hope Cove, Salcombe, Devon, 1936. Salvagers were – and are – always in hot competition to get to ships like this first.***

Left: ***The wreck of* Silvia Onarato *on Goodwin Sands in 1948. The Italian ship broke her back within eight weeks of the sinking in 1948.***

A SNAGGED AIR PIPE – AND A DIVER AND HIS DREAMS OF TREASURE ARE CONSIGNED TO OBLIVION.

The *Santa Cruz*: this Spanish treasure ship was sucked onto rocks in Cardigan Bay, just off the Pembrokeshire coast, in January 1679. The gold and silver cargo, contained in 220 chests, is worth around £40 million.

A DANGEROUS CHALLENGE

Treasure in terms of bullion and jewels is, however, not the only lure of shipwrecks. In many cases items of historic interest are just as valuable – and just as big a draw, especially if the task of recovering them is dangerous. Humphreys, for instance, has a burning ambition to recover artefacts from the *Titanic*. His plan has been to target the liner's debris field to locate, among other items, a jewel-studded copy of the *Rubaiyat of Omar Khayyam*. The project has already been swamped in legal niceties and protracted courtroom arguments.

For many wreck hunters the thrill of the dive itself is often what matters. Many rotting hulls present a dangerous challenge to those who would explore them. An air pipe can easily be snagged or pulled loose and powerful and unpredictable currents can sweep divers into oblivion before they know it. And then there's always the sharks and stingrays ...

But of all the thousands of wrecks scattered around the globe few can match one lying in the mouth of the River Thames for risk factor. Quite simply the *Richard Montgomery* carries enough high explosives to flatten the nearby town of Sheerness and shatter windows ten miles away. If she blew, her 3,172 tons of TNT would be the largest non-nuclear explosion in the history of mankind.

The *Richard Montgomery* is the only officially listed 'dangerous wreck' in British waters. Divers are banned from reaching her – though that doesn't stop them trying – and Department of Trade inspectors check the cargo every couple of years to see how stable it is.

The argument has always been that the risk involved in getting the explosives out is greater than the risk of letting them be. Over the years, though, the TNT in its waterproof casings is likely to have grown increasingly unstable.

This ship's fate was sealed on the night of 20 August 1944 as she sought a Thames

Below: ***The most famous shipwreck of them all. The magnificent* Titanic *slips beneath the waves under the gaze of her shocked survivors.***

berth en route to Cherbourg. Her draught was 31 feet and her allocated berth 24 feet at low tide. When the tide went out the *Richard Montgomery* was dumped firmly on the same sandbank where she remains to this day.

To locals the hull became something of a landmark. They sailed tourists out to it, clambered across the hull and even stripped what copper they could find. Fishermen would use it as a mooring point and a dumping ground for stray bombs pulled up in their nets. There was a nasty rumour that it had bombs on board but it wasn't until years later that the British government confirmed the truth and sealed it off.

Today the most common visitors to the hull are daredevil divers who just want to tell their friends they've brushed alongside. Government officials would rather everyone just forgot about her. No one, it seems, wants to make a decision.

Would it have been the same if she'd had bullion aboard? Would the Admiralty, the Port of London and the secretary of state for defence all have passed the buck, leaving the Department of Trade to inherit the headache?

The spectacle of landlubbers dithering and meddling in the wreck and treasure business infuriated old Roland Morris. He couldn't bear the thought of the authorities grabbing the limelight (and often the cargo as well) when they'd done nothing to advance the cause of the search itself. Unlike most of his ilk, Morris found himself in 1978 in a position to hit back.

For years he'd been hunting a wreck known in Cornwall as the *Dollar Mine*. It was thought to have been carrying 19 tons of silver coins when it sank in 1798, a hoard now worth millions. Morris found the ship somewhere off Gunwalloe, near Helston, Cornwall, but the National Trust, owner of the shoreline, immediately slapped in a claim for half of anything recovered. A livid Morris accused the Trust of seeking something for nothing and in a fit of pique abandoned his project. He swore he would take the secret of its location to the grave … and he kept his word.

Today only one man – a Scillonian who was one of Morris's helpers on the *Dollar Mine* hunt – is reputed to know the site of the wreck. To date he has kept his mouth shut.

Morris would have approved.

Above: ***The wreck of Zeebrugge ferry,* Herald of Free Enterprise*. She sunk with incredible speed after a crewman left the ship's car entrance doors open by mistake.***

FURIOUS, MORRIS SWORE HE WOULD NEVER REVEAL THE LOCATION OF THE TREASURE, AND THE GRAVE HAS KEPT HIS SECRET.

PHINEAS TAYLOR BARNUM The philosophy of humbug

With his weird and wonderful collection of freaks, his fantastic stories and his opportunistic ability to make money out of every potential disaster, Phineas Taylor Barnum really was the greatest conman on Earth.

'Roll up, roll up! See the Greatest Show on Earth. Ladies and gentlemen, I can assure you you won't be disappointed.' So the self-proclaimed 'Prince of Humbug' would pull in the crowds to gawp and stare at his circus of oddities.

Phineas T. Barnum takes a place in history as perhaps the greatest showman ever as he awed Victorian audiences with his collection of strange and wonderful freaks. The son of a storekeeper, he must have been one of the first people to recognize that any publicity is good publicity. Carefully planned campaigns ensured massive coverage of everything he did.

THE SCIENCE OF MONEY MAKING

The penny showman was known for his glib one-liners such as 'There's a sucker born every minute' and the immortal 'You can fool some of the people some of the time but you can't fool all of the people all of the time.' He even gave lectures on his ability to con the public; on a trip to England in 1858, he delivered a speech in St James's Hall, Regent Street, entitled: 'The science of money making and the philosophy of humbug.'

Barnum maintained that people wanted to have the wool pulled over their eyes, and he was more than happy to do so – for a price.

His entry into the dubious world of peepshows and freakshows happened quite by chance. Until the age of 25, Barnum tinkered about with a number of different jobs, never settling on any chosen career. He ran a newspaper, tended a bar and kept a store in his home town of Bethel, Connecticut. It was when he started

Above: ***The man-bombshell. Barnum signed this acrobat as a certain crowd puller. The man was fired out of his cannon by a spring – the explosion followed a second later.***

Opposite: ***Barnum was a natural self-publicist but even he occasionally had to resort to advertising to pull in the crowds.***

Left: ***Barnum described his elephant exhibits as 'a stupendous assemblage of titan tuskers and mammoths'.***

WHEN HIS GOLD-MINE DIED ON HIM AND WAS THEN PROVED FALSE, BARNUM LOUDLY PROCLAIMED THAT HE HAD BEEN THE VICTIM OF A HOAX.

to sell theatre tickets that he was bitten by the showbiz bug.

Barnum had learned of the existence of a wizened old negress by the name of Joice Heth, who, it was claimed, was the oldest living woman on Earth and nurse to former President George Washington. He found her being exhibited in Philadelphia and hurried to buy the rights in her as a curio. She came with ancient papers which included an original bill of sale that showed George's father Augustine Washington had bought her as a slave on 5 February 1727.

As part of her act, she rambled on about the days when she was George's nurse delving into details which included the famous cherry-tree incident. But she always baffled audiences when she referred to the tree as a peach tree. Phineas exhibited her first in Niblo's Garden in New York on 10 August 1835.

As befitted the master of hype, his entrée into the world of freakshows was accompanied by a fanfare of publicity that was to become synonymous with everything he did. He took out a series of adverts in which he claimed the old crone had been 'a member of the Baptist church for upwards of one hundred years'. The press wrote reams on the phenomenon.

Alas for poor Phineas, his new-found 'crock of gold' did not last long: the old lady died. Worse was to come when the authorities carried out an autopsy on the body and declared publicly that Joice Heth was in fact 80 years old. Quick-thinking Barnum buried her in his family plot and capitalized on her again by defending his good faith in her authenticity and claiming that HE had been the victim of a hoax! He told anyone who wanted to listen that he had been duped by both Joice Heth and her original owner, having bought her in good faith.

For the next few years following her death, Barnum was pushed to find a profitable replacement. He struggled to make ends meet with a few wild animals and acrobatic troupes. However, his fortunes took a turn for the better when he decided to go into the museum business.

In 1841 he bought Sadder's American Museum, New York, and shortly afterwards purchased its arch-rival, Peales Museum. He then merged the two.

Renamed simply the American Museum, his new venture opened early in 1842, to the delight of the curious New Yorkers who filed through its doors. It was the perfect vehicle for Barnum's ingenious hoaxes. He entertained the public with rare specimens that he claimed were true freaks of nature. There were 'Niagara Falls', a woolly horse, the bearded lady, the 'Egress' and his renowned 'Feejee Mermaid' (in reality, the upper torso of a monkey sewn onto the body of a fish).

The Museum also became one of New York's entertainment hotspots, filled with genuine museum exhibits: minerals, fossils and natural history specimens, as well as an

Below: *A press release extolling the wonderful world of Barnum.*

aquarium. Barnum built a theatre he dubbed the 'lecture room' for which over the years he sold a staggering 41 million tickets. He even brought the famous Swedish singer Jenny Lind to the USA on a concert tour in 1850.

The American Museum burned down twice but Barnum rebuilt it and carried on his strange trade until 1868, when he returned to his childhood home town of Bethel, Connecticut. There, suitably skilled in the art of humbug, he embraced the world of politics, sat in the state legislature and even ran for Congress.

THE GREATEST SHOW ON EARTH

It was while in Connecticut that he came up with his greatest idea. Teaming up with two partners, he put together the grandly titled, 'P.T. Barnum's Great Travelling Museum, Menagerie, Caravan and Hippodrome'. He called it 'The Greatest Show on Earth' and it catapulted him into the limelight he so desperately courted.

The show opened on 10 April 1871 in Brooklyn, with such sensational attractions as Siamese twins, midgets, three-legged wonders, strongmen, the Giant, the Fat Lady, the Thin Man, the Armless Wonder as well as the usual fire-eaters, sword swallowers, magicians and snake charmers.

For the next 20 years, his circus heralded the start of spring in America by kicking off its tour in Madison Square Garden.

Again his highly hyped exploits ate up acres of newspaper space. When it was remarked that he had no giraffe in his circus, he issued a press statement claiming that tragically he had been forced to feed it to the lions to keep them alive on a tough sea voyage across the Atlantic.

On one visit to England he fell in love with the Brighton Pavilion and its palatial Indian design. It perfectly reflected his own style, with its showy columns and arches, so he had a close copy built, calling it 'Iranistan'. To add to the Eastern flavour, he even arranged for an elephant to plod around in a nearby field and perform for passing train passengers by pulling a plough.

Barnum was also kept in the news by the fires that seemed to dog his business. Apart from two at the American Museum, one in 1865 and another in 1868, he also lost a menagerie of animals in a blaze in 1872, the winter quarters of his zoo in 1877 and even his Connecticut home.

Ten years after the launch of his circus, Barnum joined forces with James Bailey to form 'The Barnum and Bailey Greatest Show on Earth'. This piece of theatre was transported around America on four trains made up of 107 railroad cars, each 70 feet long.

Above: *Programmes like this helped launch Barnum's showbusiness career.*

BARNUM'S CAREER WAS DOGGED BY MYSTERIOUS – AND CONVENIENT – FIRES.

THE DIMINUTIVE QUEEN VICTORIA ADORED THE TINY MIDGET AND MADE HIM HER PET.

Right: ***Circus acts were all very well, but what the punters really wanted was freaks and plenty of 'em. Barnum never failed to impress with motley assortments such as these, and he spared no thought for the feelings of his employees. If they didn't like being dubbed 'living monstrosities' they could always seek employment elsewhere!***

Opposite below: ***P.T. Barnum with perhaps his best-known performer, 'General' Tom Thumb.***

A REAL-LIFE TOM THUMB

Yet while Barnum was an amazing self-publicist and entrepreneur, he would have been nothing without the men and women whose freakish looks helped to fill his coffers. These 'performers' became overnight stars as they fed the voracious Victorian appetite for sensation.

General Tom Thumb was the most celebrated of them all. As his name suggests, he was a man of tiny proportions yet perfectly formed. A rare find, and one Phineas Barnum put to good use.

Tom Thumb was not his real name. He was born Charles Sherwood Stratton on 4 January 1838. A healthy 9lb when he entered the world, he astonishingly remained at that weight until he was 5 years of age. He then measured a tiny 2 feet 1 inch. What made Stratton extremely unusual was that he was a true midget and not a dwarf. His body was perfectly proportioned.

His parents quickly realized the earning potential of such a Lilliputian miracle and put the lad on display, something that was seen as the norm in mawkish Victorian times. It wasn't long before Barnum got to hear of the minuscule boy on show in Bridgeport, Connecticut. He raced to sign him up and tempted him to join his circus for the princely sum of $3 a week.

Phineas immediately re-christened him General Tom Thumb and set about training the toddler in the art of showmanship. He spent days and nights schooling him in the strange ways of the peepshow world, teaching the boy to act 'regal, impudent and autocratic'.

Tom Thumb's first public appearance brought the house down when he recited a pun-littered speech written by Barnum. American audiences took to the little person Barnum hyped as a 'dwarf of 11 years of age, just arrived from England'.

The general revelled in his image as an arrogant, barking bombast. He also acted out roles such as Cupid, Yankee Doodle Dandy, Napoleon and a scantily clad gladiator.

The master showman stormed Europe. Queen Victoria, herself rather lacking in height at only 4 feet 11 inches, identified with the midget. She loved Tom Thumb and summoned him to give three Royal Command Performances at Buckingham Palace. He became known as the 'Pet of the Palace'.

Tom also proved highly popular at the Parisian court, with Barnum being allowed to exhibit his profitable protégé in a minuscule carriage in the imperial enclosure at Longchamps.

Tom Thumb's statistics were amazing enough, but Phineas Barnum, always keen to take things one step further, exaggerated Tom's age by 6 years and advertised his height at 30 1/2 inches. In fact, by the time the 'general' had reached maturity, he had attained a 'towering' 3 feet 4 inches and sported a dashing military-style set of whiskers.

Tom's marriage to midget Lavinia Warren, who stood at almost the same height as the man himself, was a showbiz affair. Barnum, ever a shrewd businessman, saw the opportunity to make an extra buck

Above: ***The train that carried Barnum and Bailey on their yearly tours.***

DESPITE THE FACT THAT HE WAS BORN WITH THREE LEGS HE MARRIED AND FATHERED FOUR NORMAL CHILDREN.

and the public went wild for his photographs of the couple's happy day.

Tom and Lavinia eventually settled down to live off the amassed fortune the couple made together – a staggering three-quarters of a million dollars. But tragically Tom fell ill and died of apoplexy back in Bridgeport at the age of 45.

A VICTORIAN FREAK SHOW

Madam Fortune, the Bearded Lady, joined Barnum and in the first nine months drew a massive 3 1/2 million paying customers. When she married and had two children her own son also became an exhibit. Given the showname 'Infant Esau', the child was born thoroughly covered in hair, with full fair-coloured whiskers. Curiously, Barnum dressed the boy in girl's clothes until he was 14 years old in the hope of hoaxing the public into believing the child was in fact a girl.

The Three-Legged Wonder, Francesco Lentini, spent time at many circuses including Barnum and Bailey's. Born in 1889 into a large family of 12 children in Rosolini, Sicily, he found it hard to cope mentally with the extra leg that grew from the right side of his body.

A visit to an institution for the severely handicapped and deformed children at the age of 7 helped him to snap out of the depression that had reached chronic levels as he became more aware of being an oddity.

Surgeons had advised his distraught parents that to try to remove it could spell instant death or paralysis. They believed that the third leg was part of an undeveloped Siamese twin. Instead of the egg dividing in two, it only partly divided, leaving Francesco with just a leg of the brother he never had, attached forever to the base of his spine.

Francesco was highly intelligent and mastered four languages. However, the only career path he could take was that of the freakshow circuit. He joined the Ringling Brothers' Circus before touring with Barnum and Bailey. Fascinated audiences gasped in wonder as he ran, jumped, rode a bicycle and horse, drove a car and even skated on ice. He became known as the 'Three-Legged Wonder', and had people in gales of laughter when he played football, having trained himself to use the middle leg to kick the ball around.

He made fun of his own disfigurement by telling people he was the only man he knew who brought his own stool everywhere with him. His sense of humour helped him through life. Once when asked how he fitted himself with shoes, he said he bought two pairs and gave the extra one to a one-legged friend.

The Three-Legged Wonder even married and had four normal children. He retired to Florida and died in 1966 at the grand old age of 77.

Barnum was famous for his frauds, but he seemed to be able to carry them off because a tolerant public found them so entertaining and elaborate. The master

Below: *Another of Barnum's personal favourites – Johanna, the intelligent gorilla. He described her as 'a stumbling block to doubters of the Darwinian theory' in an attempt to convince his public that he was truly a man of science.*

showman and trickster once presented what he claimed to be the 'Wild Men of Borneo' as proof of the missing link between man and ape.

They were a fierce-looking pair, short and squat. In fact, they were actually American-born midget brothers who had never seen a jungle in their lives. Christened Hiram and Barney Davis, they changed their names to the more showy Plutano and Waino.

Barnum did not stop there. He also showed 'Zip the Man Monkey', supposedly a savage Neanderthal creature. Although he looked like a monster from a far-flung land, with a shaven head topped with a matted knot of hair, the creature was really a poor negro simpleton child encouraged to emit growling noises to earn a few pennies.

Scotsman Angus Macaskill was born in the Outer Hebrides in 1825, where he grew to a staggering 7 feet 9 inches in his bare feet. Billed as the 'strongest man the world has ever seen', his amazing feats stood testimony to his power.

Angus started out his working life as a docker and a fisherman before going on to fame in Barnum's Greatest Ever Show. Barnum got his money's worth out of the huge man. Not only did he display his freakish strength in the circus ring, he also used him to help to erect the big top tents. The mild-mannered giant hammered thick tent-pegs into the ground using not one but two 14lb hammers – one in each hand.

Angus knew that he could kill a man with his awesome power. As he gripped one wrestling opponent's hand in a friendly gesture, the man was horrified to see blood oozing from under his fingernails.

Like General Tom Thumb, Angus Macaskill came to the attention of freakshow enthusiast Queen Victoria. In response to yet another Royal summons, Barnum took his prize 'Hercules' to Windsor Castle.

GRIPPED BY THE COLOSSAL HAND, THE MAN WATCHED HORRIFIED AS THE BLOOD OOZED FROM UNDER HIS FINGERNAILS.

Below: ***Jumbo the 'monster elephant' on his journey through New York to Madison Square Gardens for a Barnum extravaganza. The showman bought him from London Zoo but later claimed he was the only living 'mastodon'.***

LAST SIX WEEKS.

BARNUM & BAILEY

GREATEST SHOW ON EARTH.

CHANGE OF PROGRAMME. CLOSING EXHIBITIONS OF THE GRANDEST & MOST SUCCESSFUL SEASON EVER KNOWN IN OLYMPIA.

FINAL PERFORMANCES in LONDON of the BARNUM & BAILEY Greatest Show on Earth. Positively Closing the Glorious and Triumphant Sojourn

ON SATURDAY, APRIL 2.

Courier Co. BUFFALO N.Y. U.S.A. **THE ENORMOUS HORSE FAIR** SHOWING THE VAST CAVALCADE OF HIGH-CLASS STOCK OWNED & EXHIBITED BY THE GREAT BARNUM & BAILEY SHOW AN ACTUAL SCENE ON THE GREAT HIPPODROME TRACK. OVER 400 CHOICE THOROUGHBREDS FROM ALL PARTS OF THE WORLD

AND THEN TOURING THE WHOLE OF GREAT BRITAIN.
Travelling the Entire, Mighty, Undivided Show UNDER A DAILY EXPENSE OF £1500, with New Acts and New Features introduced into the already Magnificent and Stupendously large Programme of
THRILLING PERFORMANCES AND GRAND DISPLAYS.
Visiting the Provinces upon its own specially constructed 70 Railway Cars, every car nearly 60 feet long.
NEARLY A FULL MILE OF RAILWAY CARS,
And exhibiting all the myriad wonders under TWELVE ENORMOUS CANVAS PAVILIONS,
One alone of which is double the capacity of Olympia.

LAST SIX WEEKS

Of the Grandest Show ever devised by man.

Last chances of witnessing the Most Magnificent Exhibition, the ingenuity, ability, wealth, and wonderful resources of the KING OF THE AMUSEMENT WORLD, as set before the bewildered eyes of London.
CHANGE OF PROGRAMME.
NEW ACTS INTRODUCED. NEW FEATURES PRESENTED. NEW ATTRACTIONS ADDED.
New Races, new Clown Capers, new Animal Tricks. Ending the London Engagement in a blaze of glory. Eye-Feasts of Splendour and Thrilling Interest. First presentation of the Mammoth
FOUR HUNDRED BLUE RIBBON HORSE FAIR,
And numerous other remarkable features.
A VERITABLE TORNADO OF WONDERS. BEWILDERING ARRAY OF NOVELTIES,
And a very Vesuvius of Brilliant Attractions never seen here or anywhere else.
A PROGRAMME OF AMAZING EXTENT
Of startling Struggles, hotly contested Races, and Aërial and Equestrian Rivalries, carrying the spectators by storm, and wildly and enthusiastically applauded by everybody.
STUPENDOUS STRUGGLES BETWEEN CHAMPIONS.
Daring Deeds by Intrepid Gladiators. Tournaments, Games, Combats, Sports, Feats, Displays.
A Perfect Avalanche of Startling Events.
Races that enchanted Roman Senators.
Furious Two and Four-Horse Roman Chariot Races.
Bareback Equestrian, High School, Classic, Athletic, Acrobatic, Gymnastic, and Aërial Contests of all kinds, together with
TRIALS OF SKILL, ENDURANCE, AND BRAVERY,
In Three Rings, upon Two Stages, on the Race Track, in the Grand Aërial Enclave, and upon the 450-feet Spectacular Stage.
Pageants Exhausting Art and Luxury.
The whole vast space of the many Arenas a BEWILDERING SCENE OF KALEIDOSCOPIC SPLENDOUR.
REALLY THE WORLD'S SPECTACULAR SENSATION. THE MIGHTY METROPOLIS OF WONDERLAND.
The United Universal Press a Unit in its praise. Enlightenment and Science its greatest aids.
A Stupendous Place, where Wonder itself is lost in Wonder.
Volumes could not enumerate its myriad Treasures, to all of which are added the Double
MENAGERIES OF WILD AND TRAINED BEASTS.
THREE HERDS OF PERFORMING ELEPHANTS, Grand Horse Fair, Droves of Camels, Shetland Ponies, Zebras, Llamas, Alpacas, Guanacos, Tiny Zebras.
THE FAMOUS COLLECTION OF WONDERFUL FRFAKS.
Armless and Legless Men, Bearded Lady, Tattooed People, Dog-Faced Boy, Moss-Haired Girl, Expansionists, Sword Swallower, Fire King, Musical Phenomena, Egyptian Juggler, Giant, Miliget, Giantess, Fat Woman, Skeleton Dude, Laloo and Lala, Whirling Dervishes, Head Swinging Soudanese, and Others.
A PERFECT PANDEMONIUM OF ORIGINALITY AND HUMOUR
By the CLEVEREST CLOWNS IN THE WORLD.
And in wondrous addition thereto the GRAND SPECTACULAR MILITARY DRAMA of

THE MAHDI: Or, for the Victoria Cross,

With 1200 Men, Women, Soldiers, Sailors, Soudanese, Horses, Camels, &c., depicting with truth and accuracy actual events in the War in the Soudan.
AND ONE TICKET ADMITS TO ALL. TWO GRAND EXHIBITIONS DAILY at 2 and 8 p.m. Doors open at 12.30 and 6.30.

Early Gates open (Hammersmith Road) at 12 noon and 6 p.m., for 3s. seats and upwards. Early entrance fee, 6d. extra. Owing to the stupendously large show and the general magnitude of the exhibitions necessitating great preparations, the Menageries, Freak, and Horse Fair Departments can only be open from 12 to 4.15 p.m., and from 6 to 10.30 p.m. No promenade tickets sold. Every ticket entitling holder to a reserved numbered seat, and admitting to all advertised departments without extra charge.

PRICES.—Amphitheatre, 1s. and 2s.; Arena seats, 2s., 3s., and 4s.; Balcony seats, 3s.; Stalls, 5s., 7s. 6d.; Private Boxes (five and six seats), £3 3s.; Single Box seats, 10s. 6d. Special prices for Royal Box when not engaged. Children between 4 and 10 years of age half-price to all except 1s. and 2s. seats. Box-Office open from 9 a.m. to 9.30 p.m. 1s. and 2s. seats on sale only after doors open. All other seats may be booked in advance at Box-Office and at usual Libraries.

BURNED ALIVE

On his many trips to England, the master showman was a regular visitor to the London Zoological Gardens. It was on one such visit that he came to hear about an elephant for which the curators needed to find a new home. The flamboyant Barnum stepped in and bought Jumbo.

It was a decision that the zoo would live to regret. The public loved the African elephant and there were howls of outrage as the British press declared the sale an act of vandalism.

Barnum revelled in the limelight. He shipped Jumbo to the USA, avoiding taxes by saying he was going to breed from the animal. He urged the public to come and see 'The Only Mastodon on Earth'. The mastodon, a creature related to the elephant, was long extinct but Barnum never let scientific facts get in the way of a good scam.

Four years later Jumbo died in a tragic accident. The facts were straightforward enough – the animal was hit by a train – but Barnum callously manipulated the story, claiming Jumbo had died gallantly, saving a baby elephant by sacrificing himself.

Barnum needed a replacement and once again he turned to the Royal Zoological Society in London. Surprisingly, they fulfilled his order and a female, Alice, was sent to take Jumbo's place. The ambling giant was presented as the male elephant's 'widow'.

She was often displayed beside Jumbo's gruesome remains, his stuffed hide on one side and his gleaming skeleton on the other. Sadly, Alice also met a grisly end when she was burned alive in a fire in 1887.

Never the shrinking violet type, Barnum was thrilled when London's waxwork museum Madam Tussaud's asked him if he would like to be immortalized as an exhibition. The impudent entertainer sent them a complete outfit, even down to his socks. Fittingly it was in London (where he had an enormous following) that he climaxed his long career. The 'Greatest Show on Earth' went on display in the huge Olympia exhibition halls and Londoners packed in to get a glimpse of the man who was as famous as any one of his living freaks.

The egoistical Barnum had an open carriage made for him to ride around the ring before the start of the show. Once again he had royal patronage: young Prince George sat enthralled through the entire show, joyfully joining in the National Anthem which he dubbed: 'God Save Grandmother'.

Besides being a showman, Phineas became a real estate speculator. He also gave numerous lectures around the world. And as a politician he served four terms in the Connecticut state legislature before going on to become mayor of his home town, Bridgeport. Today the small town's Barnum Museum stands testimony to the greatest showman on Earth.

Although Barnum was married twice – to Charity Hallett in 1829 and a year after her death in 1873 to Nancy Fish – he never fathered any children. His showmanship went to the grave with him in 1891 at the grand old age of 81.

Ironically, the *New York Evening Post* had printed the old man's obituary days before his death and Barnum had read it. Was it his last attempt to 'plant' a story in the press? No doubt he got a great kick out of it.

ALICE MET A GRISLY END WHEN SHE WAS BURNED ALIVE IN A FIRE.

Opposite: ***A handbill from a Barnum season at Olympia. By now the master showman was as well known as any of his freaks and he revelled in the applause of an adoring public. He even had an open carriage specially made for him to ride around the ring before the start of the show.***

Left: ***The twopenny programme for Barnum at Olympia. He chose the exhibition halls to stage the climax of his career and milked every ounce of publicity from the fact that the young Prince George would be present.***

DREAM OF FLIGHT

Since time immemorial human beings have dreamed of flying like a bird, but over the centuries only lunatics and geniuses dared to attempt the impossible. Some crashed to their bloody deaths, some flew too high and were punished for their foolhardiness, and a few – a brilliant few – learned to master the last untamed element.

Like all the best dreams, this one began as an impossibility. A person to fly like a bird? Madness. The stuff of doddery inventors or good-for-nothings with little else to do.

True, the story of flight is littered with its fair share of eccentrics, optimists, con-men, opportunists and, inevitably, the downright bonkers. Yet amid all the dross that goes with any great scientific advance, there were a few jewels. Two such were the Montgolfier brothers of Avignon in France.

The Montgolfiers came into the race to get airborne on the back of a pretty grim record. Even in make-believe stories it nearly always ended in tears for the would-be flyers. The classic example is the attempt by Icarus to escape from King Minos of Crete. He glued feathers to his arms with wax and took off for home. As almost every school child knows, he flew too near the Sun, the wax melted and – whoops! – no more Icarus.

A LEAP INTO THE UNKNOWN

History is littered with the stories of men who thought this unfortunate Greek was on the right lines. They all ended up in the drink as well. There was King Bladud of London who in 852 BC became the first of the so-called tower jumpers. He jumped, he crashed, he died – but he didn't deter others from having a try as well. Across the world for nigh on a thousand years (and even today) there have been people prepared to chuck themselves off high buildings in the name of scientific progress.

There were one or two who took care to improve their chances of survival. The 'flying tailor' of Ulm, Germany, for instance, made sure he landed in the town's river. Luckily his wings kept him afloat until his derisive fellow-citizens fished him out. Then there was the intrepid Sieur Bernier, who started out by jumping off a stool and worked up, via a table and window, to the second storey of a house. There is no believable record of how his career ended.

Some of the most colourful early attempts to fly were made by monarchs, who doubtless convinced themselves God was on their side. According to the 10th-century tome *Shah-Nameh* (*King's Name Book*) of Persia, King Kai Koos had a pretty good stab with one of the most bizarre flying contraptions ever conceived.

The book records: 'To the king it became a matter of great concern how he might be enabled to ascend the heavens, without wings; and for that purpose he consulted the astrologers who presently suggested a way in which his desires might be successfully accomplished.

HE JUMPED OFF A STOOL; AND THEN OFF A TABLE; AND THEN OUT OF A SECOND-STOREY WINDOW ...

Opposite: ***The Montgolfiers' moment of triumph. This engraving shows last-minute preparations for the first free flight with the Marquis d'Arlandes and Dr Pilatre de Rozier acting as test pilots.***

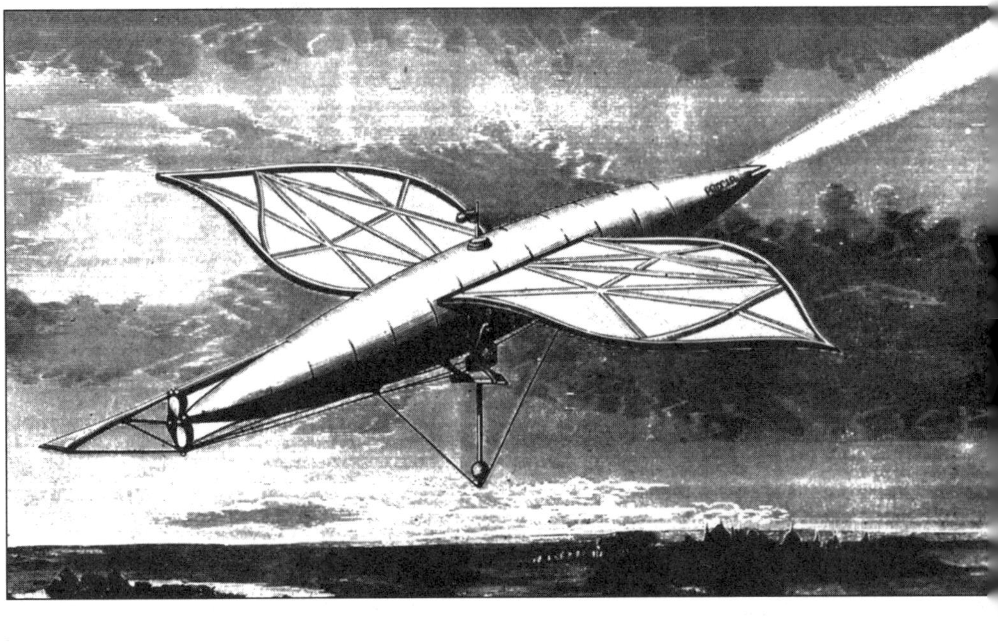

Below: ***This plan for a flying machine, dated around 1883, was drawn by inventor Professor Boronowski. It was powered by steam and far too unwieldy to be any use.***

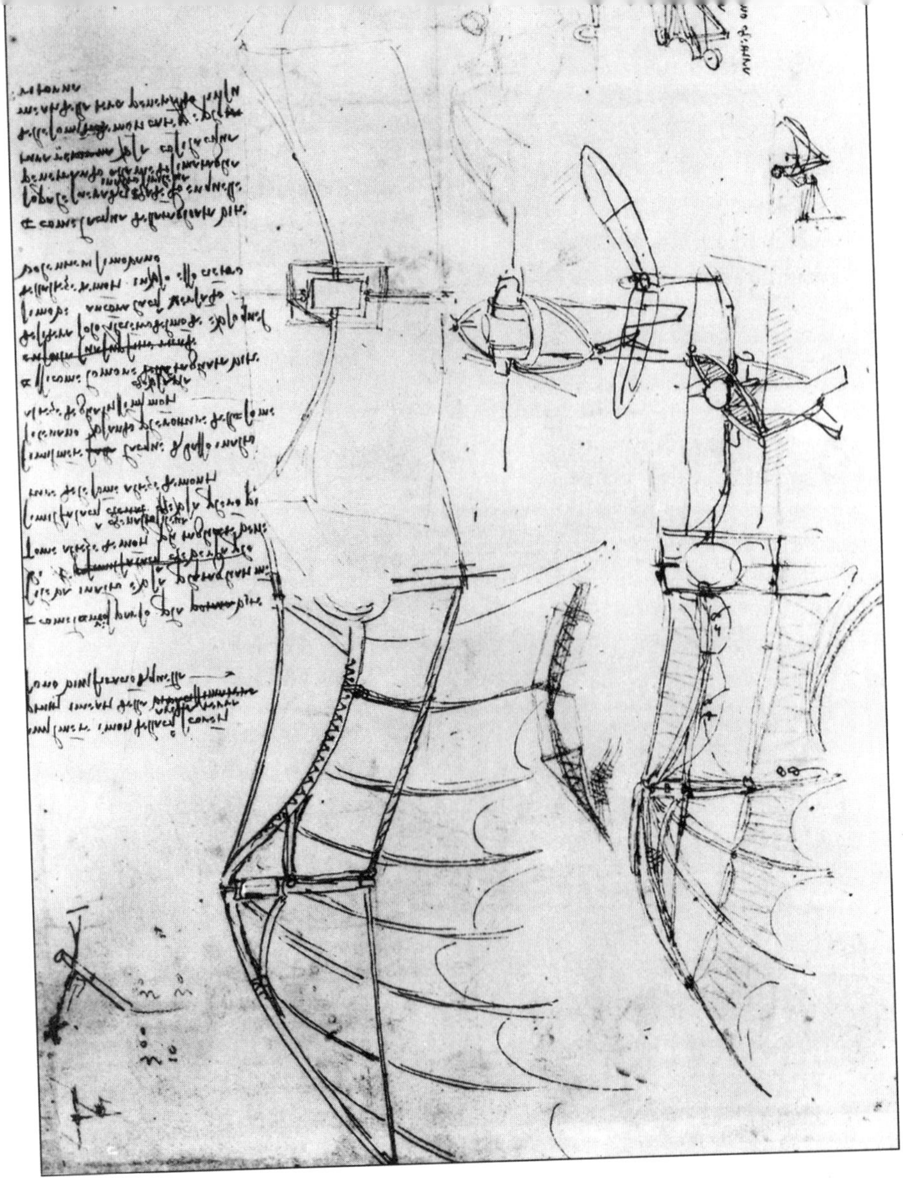

Above: ***Leonardo da Vinci's design for a fixed-wing aircraft was years ahead of its time. Whether it would actually have flown is quite another matter.***

'They contrived to rob an eagle's nest of its young, which they reared with great care, supplying them with invigorating food. A frame of aloes wood was then prepared and at each of the four corners was fixed perpendicularly a javelin, surmounted on the point with the flesh of a goat. At each corner again one of the eagles was bound, and in the middle the king was seated with a goblet of wine before him.

'As soon as the eagles became hungry they endeavoured to get at the goat's flesh upon the javelins and by flapping their wings and flying upwards they quickly raised the throne from the ground. Hunger still pressing on them, and still being distant from their prey, they ascended higher and higher in the clouds, conveying the astonished king far beyond his own country. But after a long and fruitless exertion their strength failed them and unable to keep their way the whole fabric came tumbling down from the sky and fell upon a dreary solitude in the Kingdom of Chin – where Kai Koos was left a prey to hunger, alone, and in utter despair.'

Cutting through the journalistic licence of the day, we can safely conclude that Koos bombed out.

By the 17th century the weird science mob were still in charge. Jesuit maths lecturer Francesco de Lana conceived a lighter-than-air machine hoisted aloft by four balloons and propelled by oars and a large sail. Forty years later, in 1709, another Jesuit, Father Laurenco de Gusmao of Portugal, built a flying craft he called the Passarola. It had a kind of parachute contraption above a dove-shaped hull and two large flapping wings. Neither invention could be described as successful.

Then in 1742 the Marquis de Bacqueville flew for France (almost) when he leapt out of his town house on the River Seine with huge paddles attached to his arms and legs. If he'd landed in the river the paddles might at least have been a useful buoyancy aide. As it was he plopped onto a barge and broke his leg.

A BAG OF HOT AIR?

So what of the Montgolfiers, Joseph and Etienne? In 1782, so the story goes, they were at home watching the fire when they noticed how fragments of ash swirled up the chimney. Observing correctly that warm air rises, they later launched the first, experimental hot air balloon by igniting a paper fire under an open silk bag.

A year later, in the autumn of 1783, the first documented manned flight took place with a doctor called Pilatre de Rozier in the basket. But, for safety's sake, his balloon remained tethered to the ground.

The Montgolfiers' next move was a free flight and they dutifully asked the permission of Louis XVI. He replied: 'Take two criminals who are under a death sentence and tie them to the balloon basket. That will be a novel way of disposing of worthless men.'

As it turned out the king's suggestion was shelved. A nobleman, the Marquis d'Arlandes, cajoled him into accepting it would be wrong for such a historic moment to be handed to a couple of scumbag killers. The king gave way and it was d'Arlandes and de Rozier who on 21 November 1783 made the world's first independent flight across most of Paris.

Flushed with success, de Rozier sought to break new ground. An argument was developing among prospective aeronauts over which was the more effective flier: a balloon filled with hot air or one that used the new lighter-than-air gas hydrogen, discovered in 1766 by the English chemist Henry Cavendish. The Frenchman thought the obvious solution was to combine the two. In 1785 he rigged up a 10-foot hot air balloon beneath a 40-foot hydrogen one. In doing so he also created the world's first flying bomb and doomed himself to becoming the first victim of an air crash. Science discovered hydrogen and fire don't mix.

This appalling device disintegrated in flames a quarter of an hour out on its flight path across the English Channel. The mangled bodies of de Rozier and his co-pilot were found near the seashore, about four miles from Boulogne.

In spite of numerous accidents like these, the next century saw the golden age of ballooning, while by 1794 the world's first air force unit was seen in battle as France's General Morlot directed his forces against the Austrians and Dutch at Fleurus. The first air raid followed 55 years later when the Austrian 'air force' bombed Venice with 30-pounders. And, naturally, there were some classic *Boys' Own* tales as adventurers queued up to outdo each other in the world's most fashionable form of transport.

Not least among this band were James Glaisher and Henry Coxwell of Wolverhampton, England, who took off in 1862 to see how high they could go. Without oxygen they managed the almost unbelievable altitude of 30,000 feet (nearly six miles). By then Glaisher was unconscious and Coxwell's limbs had frozen to the point of uselessness. Yet he somehow managed to grip the safety valve cord with his teeth and returned safely to Earth.

THE BATTLE FOR THE SKIES

By now science had switched its attentions to gliders as a possible way forward for powered flight, and once the petrol engine appeared in 1885 whole new avenues began to open up.

In 1900 bicyclemakers Wilbur and Orville Wright of Dayton, Ohio, produced a biplane glider which they tested in the form of a gigantic kite over the sands at Kitty Hawk, North Carolina. Three years (and much experimentation) later they finally strapped a homemade 12 hp motor on it and on 17 December Wilbur flew the contraption for 59 seconds over 300 yards. Within two years they'd redesigned the aircraft to the point where it could manage 24 miles in 38 minutes.

The age of powered, manned flight had arrived ... and with it a whole new band of enthusiastic fruitcakes set on getting their names in the history books. Incredibly dozens got their batty ideas commissioned – very often by the paranoid military hierarchies of Britain and Germany who in 1914 were busy squaring up for the first test to decide which of them was master of Europe.

On the German side Villehad Forssman (he was in fact a Swede but he was happy to work with anyone mad enough to pay him) was one of the great optimists of the story of flight. As a designer he was so bad the British should have decorated him for the trouble he caused their enemy.

Forssman's only qualification, it seems, was that he once built a monoplane called the Bulldog for Prince Friedrich Sigismund. On the strength of this, and some earlier tinkering with dodgy airships in Russia, he was taken on by the German aircraft company Siemens.

Above: ***The Chanute multiple-wing glider is put through its paces in 1896. By now scientists had realized that fixed wings were the way forward to powered flight and the arrival of the internal combustion engine had opened up undreamt-of opportunities.***

TO PROVE HIS ARGUMENT HE TESTED HIS THEORY – AND CREATED THE WORLD'S FIRST FLYING BOMB.

Any entrepreneur will tell you it is very hard to lose money making much-in-demand military hardware in times of war. Yet Siemens managed it (certainly in the early stages of hostilities), largely because Forssman talked them into building Bulldogs. The German generals were desperate for planes ... but not that desperate.

Above: ***A classic in the ranks of weird and wonderful aeroplanes that never stood a chance. This is the Avion Ader built in 1890. Amazingly, there was no shortage of test pilots volunteering to try it out.***

Forssman then turned his attention to producing the world's first seriously efficient bombers and came up with a giant flying pig of a plane that was too heavy in some parts, too weak in others, and carried engines that were hopelessly under-powered. He solved the problem of the tail section's excess weight by bunging a gunner's turret on the nose of the thing. Unsurprisingly, it was completely unfit to fly.

Siemens dumped the Swede and employed an engineer called Harold Wolff to salvage something from the wreckage. He failed – even though he had an ace pre-war test pilot, Walter Hohndorf, at the controls – and in 1915 the whole unwieldy mishmash crashed during a brief hop off the ground. Unfortunately it wasn't quite a write-off. Siemens, by now getting desperate for a return on their Deutschmarks, vowed they would get the thing accepted by the military somehow.

A deal was struck. The generals would take the plane into service (at a reduced purchase price) if it managed to achieve a height of 6,000 feet in under half an hour and could carry a 1,000 kg payload for four hours. Siemens wheeled out another pilot, Bruno Steffen, and promised him a 10 per cent cut if he could coax the monster through its paces.

Steffen agreed and asked for five volunteers to make up his load. There were no takers. Undeterred, and packed up with ballast, he took off to quickly find the plane was so heavy it flew under constant risk of either stalling, spinning or rearing up on its tail like some bellyflopping whale. He managed to make 6,000 feet with little over 100 seconds to spare but on the way down all four engines failed. Steffen, clearly a brilliant airman, glided the machine down for a textbook landing.

The military engineers moved in, checked instruments, pronounced the test successful and sentenced a whole new intake of fresh-faced recruits to use the flying coffin for 'training purposes'. Thankfully fate intervened in time.

Shortly after Steffen's epic performance the bomber was being tested by ground crew with its engines running when the fuselage suddenly snapped in two just behind the wings. It was the last straw and the plane was junked for good.

Not so its creator Forssman. Although little is known of him after his Siemens fiasco it appears he did find some other monumentally clueless backer who allowed him to mash together yet another winged nightmare. Soon after the Armistice an Allied Control Commission team discovered purely by chance in a dusty old hangar a partly-constructed triplane of incredible dimensions.

It had a wingspan of 165 feet, a length of 150 feet, and landing wheels 8 feet in diameter. There were to have been ten engines and it could supposedly carry enough fuel to keep it airborne for three days, during which time it would have flown to New York to drop propaganda leaflets.

The designer's name was noted as Forstman – almost certainly a misspelling. No other aircraft maker would dared have build something so huge with a structure so ludicrously weak. Thankfully it never even got out of its hangar, let alone taxied down a runway.

TARRANT'S FOLLY

Lest for a moment it be thought the British were above such foolhardy ventures, there is one outstanding case which easily rivals Forssman's fudges. Step forward W.G. Tarrant of Byfleet, Surrey, a man whose dalliance with aeroplanes proved a predictable triumph of natural law over unnatural optimism.

Tarrant's background was in building, particularly wooden buildings. In the early days of World War 1 a lot of business came his way from the War Office (in common

THE FLYING COFFIN WAS PRONOUNCED A SUCCESS AND ANOTHER INTAKE OF FRESH-FACED RECRUITS WAS FED TO IT.

Below: ***Now we're getting somewhere. This picture shows the Wright brothers' first powered flight on 17 December 1903. They managed to travel a mere 300 yards in 59 seconds. Two years later the plane notched up one flight of 24 miles in 38 minutes.***

THE PLANE WAS NOSE HEAVY AND HAD A TENDENCY FOR THE TAIL TO SHOOT UP IN THE AIR, BUT THE TEST PILOT HAD NO CHOICE.

with just about every other carpenter in the land able to wield a chisel). So it was that when the government sent out a clarion call for anyone able to design a really monstrous bomber he decided to have a go. There were only two designers in the running: Fred Handley-Page, who had built thousands of planes in his time, and Tarrant, who hadn't. Not even one.

Sure enough, bearing in mind the cock-up theory of war, the government's own Royal Aircraft Establishment at Farnborough came down on Tarrant's side. He was invited to build a 'bloody paralyser', a craft that could pack such a payload as to rain havoc on Berlin. It would be sweet revenge for the German bombing of London with Zeppelin airships.

As it turned out, Tarrant's Tabor was never ready to fly in anger, but by the end of the war the RAE had become so involved in the project they had almost adopted it. The decision was made: the Tabor would be finished and even if there were years of peace ahead it could always be turned into a passenger plane.

In early spring 1919 it was wheeled out for the attentions of the press and got some rave reviews. But many were puzzled by the engine set-up of the triplane – four between the bottom and middle wings and two between the middle and top. Far from being a startling innovation of design this crackpot arrangement had been the result of necessity. The 600 hp Siddeley Tiger engines hadn't produced the goods expected of them. Where originally the plane should have carried four, it now had to have six. There was only one place to put them ... so onto the top wings they went.

When questioned about this Tarrant's team had an instant answer. Yes, you would normally expect engines in that position to bring the tail of the plane up and send the entire machine out of control. But they had worked out all the figures and the downdraught from the top wing would be sure to keep the tail firmly in place. They probably had a point, and if the plane had ever managed to take off they might even have proved it. But while their theory no doubt worked for a Tabor in flight, no one seems to have checked what problems taxiing at low speed might bring.

On 26 May the Tabor, more than 37 feet high with an incredible wingspan of 131 feet, was towed out for its first test flight. As the world prepared to quake at this latest display of awesome military power from the British, there were behind the scenes rows going on at Farnborough. Tarrant was worried about the balance, the RAE wasn't. Tarrant took the initiative and ordered half-a-ton of lead to be packed into the nose. Now he had a plane which was nose heavy, with a tendency for the tail to shoot up in the air.

As the last of the six engines was finally coaxed into action, test pilot Captain F. Dunn took over for the inaugural flight. He taxied about for a while to get the feel of the controls and then turned into the wind for take-off. He opened up the lower engines – no problem there. Then he throttled the two top ones. Immediately the Tabor toppled nose forward, her propellors ripping up the earth and tearing the hull to pieces. All three captains on board died, though three RAE engineers were saved.

Tarrant's folly never left the ground. He went back to building houses.

At least the Tabor never got accepted as a front-line plane. Unfortunately, military history is littered with anecdotes of undeniably bad aircraft that did.

BLOODBATH

One of these is the Brewster Buffalo, used extensively by the Americans in World War 2 against the far superior Japanese Zero fighters. Stories of its inadequacies are legion. On one occasion it was claimed Brewsters were sent up to escort a squadron of fully loaded Blenheim bombers. Embarrassingly, the Brewsters couldn't keep up.

Then there was the story of a US pilot who was visiting an RAF base in Rangoon. Among its aircraft the RAF had two of the US fighters. The American casually asked what the procedure was for warning of a Japanese air raid. 'Long before the RAF gets around to announcing an alert,' he was told 'you will see two Brewsters taking off in a westerly direction regardless of the windsock. That's the signal. The Japanese always fly in from the east.'

The Brewster's problem was that it was heavy on armour plate, light on firepower. As a result US pilots got planes that were easily out-manouevred by the Japanese and

rarely able to get a shot on target. In one of the worst bloodbaths, during the Midway Battle of 4 June 1942, a US Marine squadron put up 25 fighters (including 19 Brewsters) against 36 Zeros escorting a fleet of bombers.

Inside half an hour, 13 of the Brewsters were shot down and the rest were so badly damaged they were never used again. A Captain Philip White, who did get his plane home, observed later: 'It is my belief that any commander who orders pilots out for combat in a Brewster should consider the pilot as lost before leaving the ground.' Australian airmen would no doubt agree. They were given 154 Brewsters to help defend Malaya. Inside three months every one was destroyed.

Even when this hapless fighter chanced upon sitting targets – a so-called duck shoot – it couldn't perform. One flight log showed that three Brewsters managed to intercept an unprotected flight of Japanese bombers. Then the crews found that out of a combined total of 12 guns, only one actually worked.

A SUICIDE MACHINE

If the Brewster was too slow, the German ME-163 Komet proved too fast. In 1941 this tiny rocket-powered interceptor achieved a test speed of 600 mph, an unimaginable speed by the standards of the day. Intelligence reports of its existence had been one of the biggest headaches for Allied air commanders. In fact, it is likely the Komet accounted for more German casualties than it inflicted upon the enemy.

The Komet worked using a highly unstable rocket fuel mixture of C-Stoff (a solution of hydrazine hydrate in methanol) and T-Stoff (hydrogen peroxide with a few – laughingly named – stabilizers). No

Above: ***The* Hindenburg *disaster, on 6 May 1937. This terrifying photograph showing the scenes that day in New Jersey sums up the spirit of the early aviators. For all their bravado, many knew in their hearts that they were dealing with technology still in its infancy.***

Above: ***Another of the early gliders takes off with its brave test pilot hanging on for dear life. For the men who did manage to get themselves airborne, there was the obvious problem of how and where to land. Without controls, they quite literally flew on a wing and a prayer.***

ignition was needed. As soon as the two fuels met, they transformed into an explosive hot gas, a feature that accounted for more than one unfortunate ground crew member who slopped one of the fuels into a bucket containing dregs of the other.

Its only chance of operating effectively was for everything to be kept as simple as possible. And it was. The pilot had only five engine controls: off, idle, and thrusts 1, 2 and 3. Recruits were prepared for the terrifying G-forces it created by being locked into a pressure chamber and exposed to the agonies of rising to 24,000 feet in a minute and back down to sea-level in half that time.

One would-be Komet pilot wrote later: 'Our bowels felt as though they were expanding like balloons, forcing us to scream with agony, while if we happened to be suffering with a slight head cold and a blocked sinus these sudden pressure changes resulted in such searing head pains that the agony was indescribable.'

Only volunteers were accepted for 163 Squadron and it's easy to understand why. The engine could explode, at any time, without any warning or any apparent reason. Death was then guaranteed instantaneous. You took off on a wheeled trolley but often as not this gave the motor such a jolt that it would cut out on the point of take-off. Landing was even more haphazard because the plane landed like a glider on a single undercarriage skid. The main difference was that a glider can come down as slow as 30 mph: a Komet was supposed to do it at 100 mph.

Crash landings on both take-off and landing were, therefore, an everyday occurrence, as was steam spurting into the cockpit to obscure vision completely. The only advice if anything, however minor, went wrong was to bale out and hope you didn't get sliced in half by the tail fin on the way. The pilots who knew they were about to crash probably prayed for an explosion. On occasions a Komet would come down with just one ruptured fuel tank and the pilot could then suffer the appalling fate of being dissolved alive.

Yet all these risks were somehow worth it to the brave young souls whose dream of flight was to be the fastest men on Earth. It was ironic that in military terms, their aircraft was a total dud.

The Komet came upon its targets (usually US Flying Fortresses) so quickly the pilot had time to squeeze off only a few rounds before he shot past and found himself out of range again. Assuming he had the fuel to make another run, he would be forced to throttle back, losing his one great advantage – speed. An added problem was the return home. US Mustang fighters took to patrolling close to known Komet bases, picking off the fighters with ease as they glided down.

Despite all the plane's faults the rocket technology used impressed the conquering Allies and, no doubt, inspired more scientists into pushing back the frontiers of flight.

TAKE-OFF INTO THE UNKNOWN

Today, the Americans are known to have developed a top-secret reconnaissance plane that makes the Komet look positively snail-like. The Aurora aircraft uses a ramjet engine capable of taking it from London to New York in a little over 40 minutes. From take-off it can fly to anywhere in the world inside three hours. And the chances of any enemy shooting it down are too remote to even bother about. No bullet, no missile and certainly no other plane can catch it.

Thank goodness the world has scientists who dream. In under 200 years they have helped shepherd mankind from widespread disbelief that flight would ever be possible, to that first tentative take-off in a balloon and on to planes such as the Aurora.

Today there are those who insist inter-galactic travel is never on the cards. We could never reach the speeds required, they argue, never live long enough to see new worlds.

As the dream of flight proves, never say never.

THE AGONY WAS INDESCRIBABLE.

Below: ***A Bleriot-style monoplane. Aircraft such as this may have looked as though the slightest gust of wind would blow them into matchwood, but many were surprisingly sturdy. The problem for the pilot, apart from keeping the thing under control with only basic equipment, was to counter the biting cold.***

THE PSYCHIC DETECTIVES

Officially the police don't like to confess to it, but it happens more and more. An unsolved murder, a missing work of art, or an undiscovered corpse – when their investigations are fruitless, the officers of the law pick up their telephones and ask for the assistance of the psychic detectives.

Above: ***The Vermeer painting stolen from Kenwood House in London. Nella helped police find the culprits and the psychic information she passed to detectives was so uncannily accurate that they wondered whether she was a member of the gang.***

Nella Jones walked to the bottom of the stairs. The whole world began to spin as she felt a sharp blow to the back of her head. She grabbed the banister to stop herself from falling. Terrible pain wracked her body and fear welled up inside her as she relived the final moments of an old lady's life only seconds before she was brutally murdered.

Nella, one of the world's foremost psychics, had been called in by police who needed help over an unsolved murder. A 75-year-old grandmother had been bludgeoned to death. The famous psychic had been called out of the blue by two detectives working on the murder case in only one of many occasions that she had been asked to use her special skill to help solve crimes.

Affectionately known as 'Witchy-poo' by police, Nella's discoveries as she steps back in time can never be used as evidence in a court of law. And police are often reluctant even to admit that they join forces with psychics.

When Nella, a grandmother from Bexleyheath, Kent, is called to assist, she 'becomes' the person involved in the crime, living each step of the events as they unfold. Often she takes on the person's mannerisms and voice. It was because of this that she was feeling the pain of the frail victim so acutely at the spot where the old woman was murdered …

Detectives had first contacted Nella two days earlier. They had visited her and had sat down at her dining table. Before they even had a chance to tell her who had been killed, Nella was able to give them the name of the poor woman and the names of two of the men the police had interviewed in connection with the horrific slaughter. She also described in minute detail the place where the grandmother met her death, including the furniture in the rooms.

Now she was standing in the very spot where the old lady was found dead. Nella felt ill. Working on murder cases always left her exhausted and disturbed. It would take many days before she would begin to recover from the trauma of working on such a violent crime.

Nella could 'hear' the woman's piteous cries: 'Somebody help me'. As she looked at the floor she could 'see' the woman. Known only as Mrs Box, the old lady stumbled into the living room, knocked to the floor by blows rained down on her by the callous murderer before he snatched a necklace from her neck. The pain was excruciating and the fear that she felt was paralyzing. Nella gasped. The psychic described the necklace to the police and later, once she had left the house, told them how the man had split the old lady's ear when he ripped out her earrings and how he had crushed her fingers so that they were black and blue.

Nella and the detectives returned to an unmarked police car, and she led them to a restaurant often visited by the man whom

SHE COULD HEAR THE OLD WOMAN'S PITEOUS CRIES, PLEADING FOR HELP.

Opposite: ***Peter Sutcliffe with wife Sonia. The brutal acts of the Yorkshire Ripper made Nella Jones a household name after police turned to her for advice on catching their man.***

Above: ***Police hunt for clues after another brutal Ripper murder. Officers quickly realized they were dealing with one of the worst serial killers on record but for months they failed to make any breakthrough. Then Nella had a vision of him while sipping a cup of tea with a WPC friend.***

she believed was the killer. Further along the road she pointed out a car she said was the same type the man drove. She also accurately predicted that the man worked in Dover and that he had dropped something at the scene of the crime.

When police eventually arrested the man and charged him with murder, they confirmed that everything Nella had described had been correct. As usual, she had been uncannily accurate.

TERRIFYING POWERS

Nella was born on 4 May 1932 into a family of Romany gypsies. As a child, she hid her psychic powers from everyone because she was terrified of being called a witch. It wasn't until she was 42 years old that she decided to make a career out of her talent as a clairvoyant after lying weakened and ill from overwork through her attempts to build up a cleaning business. Since then, she has built up an international following and is recognized not only for her psychic powers and ability to 'see' into the future and past, but also for her work as a healer.

For all the sterling work psychics like Nella and others have done to help combat crime and solve cases, the police are reluctant to acknowledge that they use mediums. An admission would be seen as a slur on their ability as police officers. The official line is that they are willing to take information from any source in the hope that it leads to the arrest and conviction of criminals. Usually psychics are called in when the case has reached rock-bottom and police have nowhere else to go.

Nella has worked with police forces for almost 20 years. She made her debut as a psychic detective when she told police where to find a rare stolen painting worth £2 million. The painting by Vermeer had been stolen by thieves from Kenwood House in London. Nella was watching a news report when she suddenly had a vision of where it was. She sketched out a map as the information came flooding into her mind, then rang the hotline set up by police.

Within hours, Nella was taken to Hampstead police station where she was grilled by two detectives. They took her to Kenwood and the three of them walked through the huge grounds until Nella led them to the spot where a burglar alarm lay hidden in the grass. Even the sniffer dogs had failed to find it. She also pinpointed the whereabouts of the huge gilt frame that was now empty of the painting 'The Guitar Player'.

When she returned to the incident room,

she met the man in charge of the investigation, Chief Superintendent Arthur Pike who, heartened by her success, asked her to lead on. She next took the detectives to the famous Highgate Cemetery, resting place of Karl Marx and a host of other illustrious names. On her way there she sketched the face of a man whom she said was the culprit.

As the three arrived at the gates to the cemetery, Nella immediately felt the man's presence. He was still there and had the priceless painting with him in the ancient catacombs. The two detectives left her to search the area, but she came back empty-handed.

As they left the graveyard, they showed the gatekeeper Nella's drawing. He immediately recognized the man as a well-known graverobber who was on police records. A quick comparison with a mugshot back at the station confirmed this.

By now the police were astonished at the accuracy of Nella's information, so much so that they even had her telephone tapped, just in case she may have been involved with the theft. It didn't help allay their fears when Nella accurately predicted the arrival of every ransom letter and their contents.

Not long after the first flurry of ransom notes, one of which even contained a piece of the painting, the desperate thieves got in touch threatening to burn the picture if the ransom wasn't paid. All involved were horrified at the prospect, but Nella knew the painting would be found safe and sound in a cemetery, as she had predicted all along. Not long after, it was discovered in a graveyard beside St Bartholomew's Hospital in London.

THE YORKSHIRE RIPPER

It was through her work on the Yorkshire Ripper case that Nella became a household name. Peter Sutcliffe was eventually jailed for life in 1981 for the gruesome murders of 13 women.

Nella had been having visions of the evil Ripper at odd times throughout the day. His wickedness pervaded her life and she felt frightened by the man. But it wasn't until

THE EVIL OF THE MAN STAINED HER LIFE AND SHE WAS HAUNTED BY VISIONS OF THE GRUESOME MURDERS.

Below: ***Public pressure for the Ripper to be brought to book was intense – hence the willingness of detectives to try anything that might help. When conventional methods – such as the murder re-construction performed by this WPC – failed, they turned to psychics.***

SHE FELT THE KILLING URGE RISING IN HIM DAYS BEFORE HE TOOK HIS NEXT VICTIM, BUT SHE WAS POWERLESS TO STOP HIM.

Below: ***The Yorkshire Ripper's 13th victim – Jacqueline Hill of Leeds – who was found dead on 17 November 1980. The killing gave Nella a vital clue.***

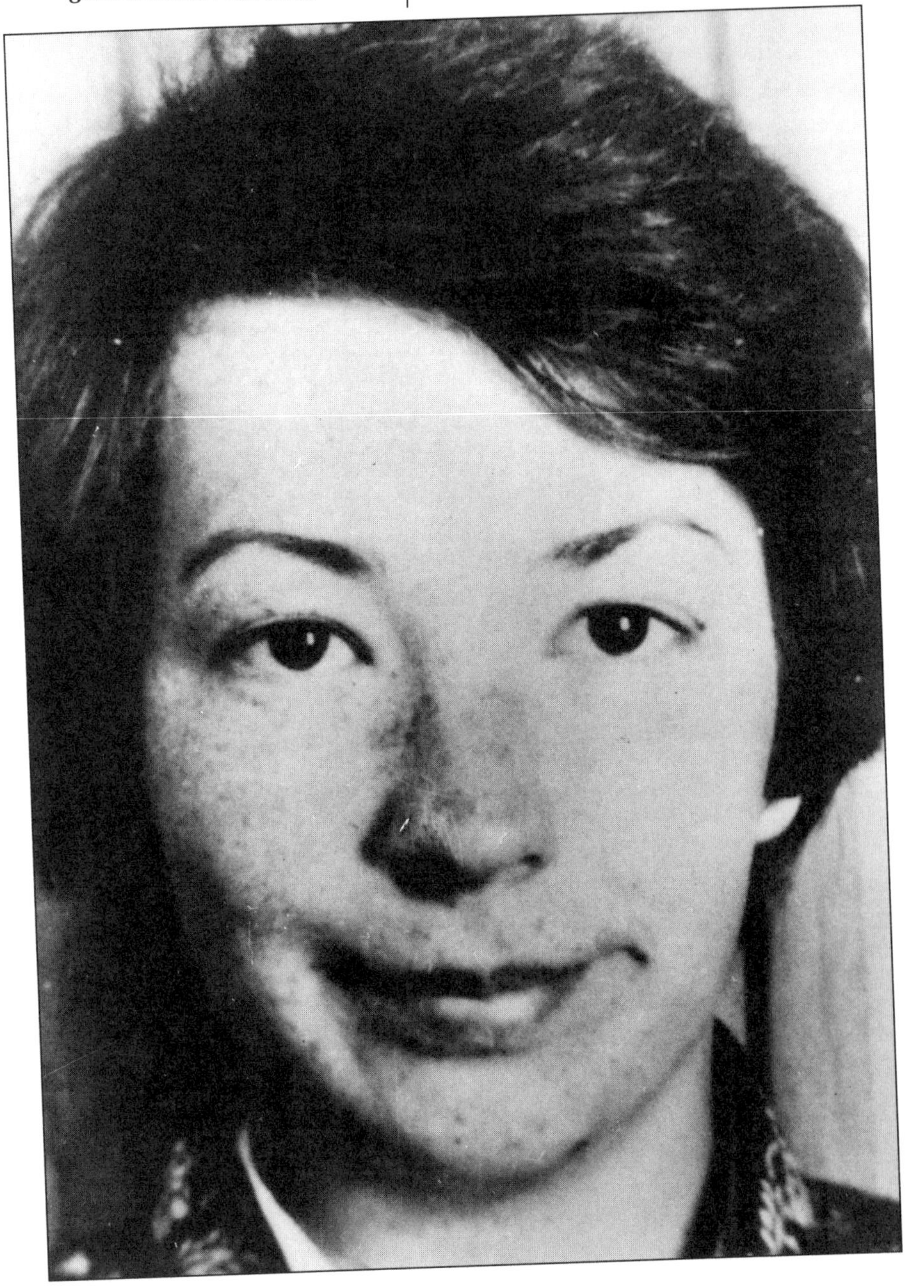

she was having a cup of tea with a policewoman friend that she became involved publicly in the hunt for the murderer. As she sat sipping the warm brew, she suddenly had a vision of him with his bag full of tools near a cemetery, and as he walked down the road she described the surrounding countryside as though looking through his dark eyes.

The policewoman immediately recognized the scene as being a place near where she used to live in Yorkshire. Shortly afterwards Nella was phoned by Shirley Davenport, who worked on the *Yorkshire Post* and had come to hear of her powers. The journalist asked her if she could give an accurate description of the murderer, who by now had been dubbed by the press the 'Yorkshire Ripper'.

Suddenly a man's face appeared in front of Nella. It hovered in mid-air just inches away from her, close enough for her to smell his bad breath and see the drops of perspiration on his skin. His eyes were blank and dark, like a shark's, and he had a fine white line above his lip and a dark beard. Nella relayed all this over the phone to the reporter until she could no longer bear to look at the vision.

She chillingly predicted that he would kill again and she described his next victim, even down to the clothes she wore. By now he had already killed 11 women and was Britain's most wanted man.

Through Shirley, Nella released as much information on the case as she was fed by her psychic powers. It took over her life for the next year: Sutcliffe's face haunted her almost daily. She also suffered horrific nightmares during which she saw him stalking women.

Throughout 1979 Nella put together the profile of the Ripper which was to prove amazingly accurate when they eventually captured the pervert.

She 'saw' that he was a long-distance lorry driver whom she was convinced lived in Bradford and was much older than the police thought.

When detectives handed her a photocopy of a letter they believed was written by the serial killer, she was immediately surrounded by a cacophony of voices who shouted the name 'Peter' over and over again. The voices instructed her to draw what they described, and she worked quickly, sketching a road with a flyover across it, a lorry depot and tall tower shaped buildings. She could see the initial 'C' on the side of the lorries. The names of two streets cropped up, Chapel Street and Charles Street.

She knew he was going to kill again, and the word 'Ainsworth' had something important to do with it. Shortly afterwards, the body of a naked young woman was found in the grounds of a house owned by a man called Peter Hainsworth. She had been strangled.

Every time the Ripper decided to kill, Nella could feel the urge rising in him in the days before he took his latest victim. Before he murdered his final victim, she accurately

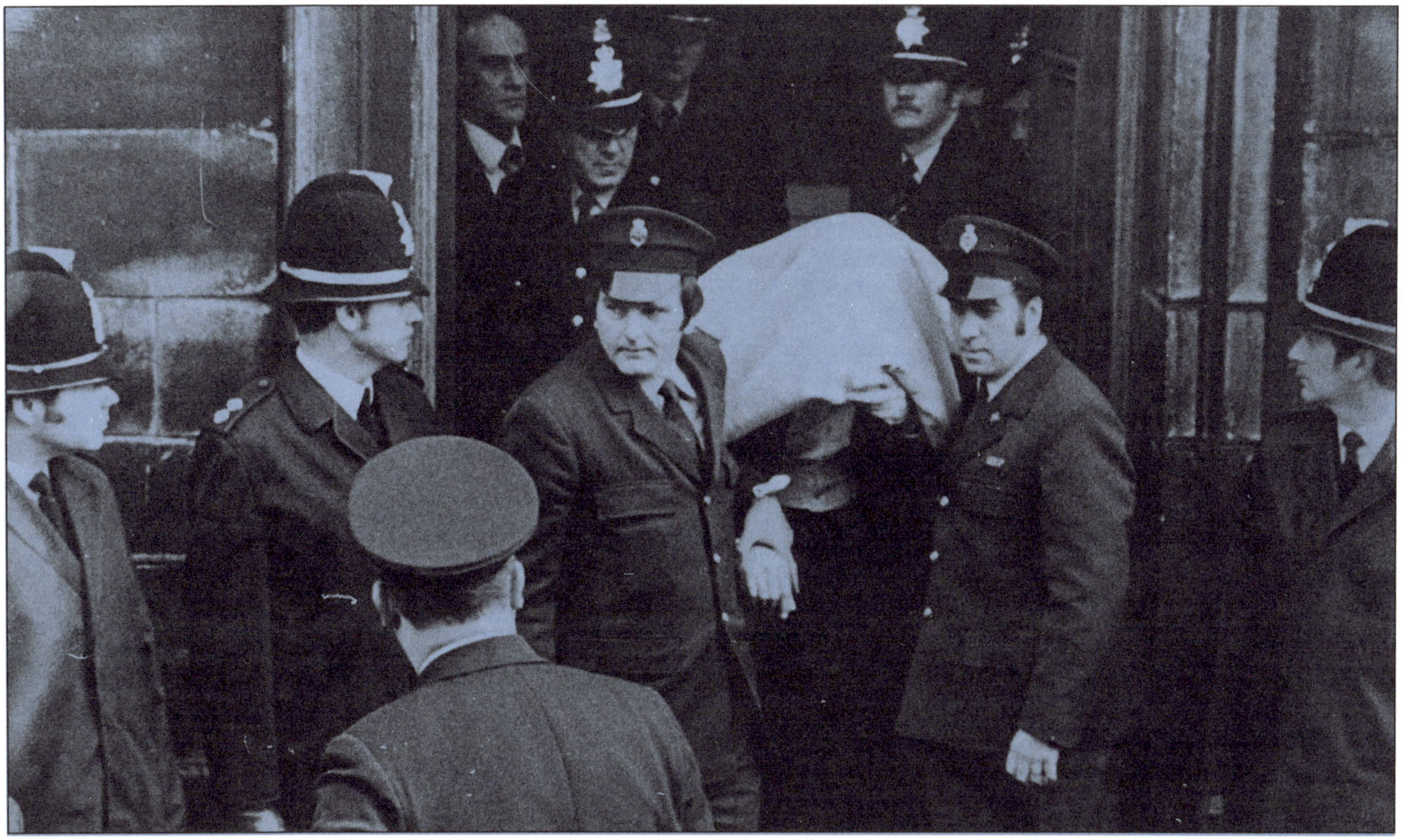

saw that the poor woman's initials were 'J.H.'. She also knew it was going to be his last murder, and that soon after he would be caught.

On 17 November 1980 the Yorkshire Ripper murdered Jacqueline Hill in Leeds. Later, as Nella retraced his steps on the day of the murder, she found the street the spirit voices had told her about: Chapel Street. It was down this street that she found a bundle of papers which she passed on to the investigating officers. She was later told they contained pictures of naked women and one had a childish drawing of a man stabbing one of the women in the heart with a knife.

Not long before Christmas 1980 Nella had a vision that the Ripper would be caught very soon. She was relieved to hear that he was arrested by police on 3 January 1981.

As Nella's fame grew, so too did the demands on her time. Once she foresaw a double murder in Brighton. A man and a woman would be found dead in a flat above an antique shop. She vividly described how the couple were in a bedroom when another man suddenly entered wielding a knife. The victims were both drunk and the woman was out cold. After a terrible struggle both lay dead, the walls awash with blood.

When she told her local police contacts, they called their colleagues in Brighton and were told that there had been no such murders in the Sussex resort. It wasn't until two months later that two charred bodies were dragged from the smouldering remains of an antique shop exactly as Nella predicted.

STARTLING ACCURACY

Nella Jones is far from being the only psychic detective in Britain …

Anne Owen, a round-faced pleasant woman with an easy smile and laughing eyes, has also been called in by police to help with their cases. She has used her clairvoyance skills to find missing persons and dead bodies. In one case, she located the whereabouts of a man who had been missing for three months. When his body was found, he had been eaten by foxes.

Anne tunes into the events surrounding the crime almost like a radio station and is into the very heart of the person who has committed the deed.

Her first big murder case was the slaying of a nurse based at a hospital in Ashford, Kent. Anne walked through the hospital corridors trying to pick up information with

Above: ***Britain's most wanted man is finally brought to justice on 3 January 1981. After successfully eluding police for so long, the Ripper's reign came to an end suddenly, taking Fleet Street and TV by surprise. Nella says she had known since well before Christmas that the hunt for him was almost over, even though the arrest had a large element of luck.***

THE RESCUE TEAM ABANDONED THEIR SEARCH BUT THE PSYCHIC KNEW THAT THREE MEN WERE STILL TRAPPED IN THE HULL OF THE BOAT.

her psychic antennae. As she explored she 'reconstructed' the crime in her mind's eye. Anne felt that the body of the slaughtered nurse was not on the premises and that it would be found elsewhere. Not long after, it was discovered just as she had foretold: wrapped in a black bag in Epping Forest after being moved there in the boot of a car. A hospital porter was later convicted of the murder.

Anne's talents have taken her abroad to solve crimes. When a young student was killed in Wiesbaden, Germany, Anne told police who the murderer was.

After the Zeebrugge ferry sank with many dead, Anne helped to save the lives of three men. Divers had abandoned their search for survivors in the cold, murky water, convinced that they had managed to rescue all of those who had not been killed. But Anne knew there were people trapped in the hull of the boat. She 'saw' three men who were miraculously still alive and quickly rang a contact at the BBC TV station who got a message through to the rescue teams. The men were found inside the ship, their lives saved by an air bubble.

Like Nella, Anne also received messages about Peter Sutcliffe as he carried out his grisly crimes. She 'saw' him as a lorry driver living in Bradford five months before his capture.

Some psychic detectives regard maps as a vital tool of the trade: the American Greta Alexander helped find the body of a young woman, Mary Cousett, simply by floating her hand above one. Mary had gone missing

Below: *The wreck of the passenger ferry* **Herald of Free Enterprise** *lies just off the coast of Zeebrugge. Three survivors owe their lives to Anne Owen's visionary abilities.*

after leaving her Illinois home with her boyfriend. She was thought to have been murdered, but police had drawn a blank when it came to finding a corpse. True, the boyfriend had been arrested and charged with her murder. Because of lack of evidence, however, the police could not bring the case to court.

As a final desperate measure they called in Greta, who concentrated on a map and told them to look in an area they had not previously searched. She also told them that the person who found the body would have a crippled hand. The body would be found in three pieces, the head and feet separated from the main torso. The letter 'S' would also be significant, she predicted. The body was found by a young policeman whose name was Steve and who had badly damaged his fingers in an accident earlier.

Nancy Czetli was called in by Maryland police to help solve the murder of 62-year-old stabbing victim, Leonetta Schilling. Nancy was shown police photo files and she picked out the picture of someone whom she believed was the killer. She said he had the same thought pattern as the murderer and predicted that police would find that Leonetta had been his babysitter at one point.

Nancy was startlingly accurate: she had chosen a picture of the old woman's nephew. Allen Glenn Finke was convicted of the brutal murder of Leonetta, who had indeed babysat for him when he was a child.

CAUGHT OUT

Sometimes psychic powers can backfire on both the medium and those who call for help. Poor Etta Louise Smith, an aircraft factory worker, had a vision in which she saw the dead body of a young woman. She rang the police and told them that she had 'seen' the corpse of a nurse who had gone missing the night before. It had been dumped in a canyon.

Etta told officers that she thought the nurse had been raped and that the killer had dealt her a fatal blow to the back of the head. Instead of heeding her warning, sceptical police arrested Etta on suspicion of murder. They had not released any details of the killing at that time, and concluded that she must have slain the nurse herself.

Etta was held for four days before three men were charged with the killing. Later she was awarded $24,000 compensation from the Los Angeles police for wrongful arrest.

Owen Etheridge, meanwhile, was caught out when he rang a psychic radio broadcaster in California. He told Dixie Reterian that his father was missing and emotionally asked her if she could help find him.

Owen was told to come into the radio station with something belonging to his father. He handed over the man's watch and ring. As he did so, Dixie looked at the teenager's face and had a vision that he had killed his father.

She called the police and told them she believed Owen had shot his father and that the body would be found nearby wrapped in a green sheet and with a green cloth tied around its neck. A detective confronted Owen with these details and the boy broke

Above: ***Sutcliffe's job as a lorry driver gave him the perfect cover to carry out his appalling crimes. No one thought it odd that he was away from home for long periods of time and Sutcliffe would while away the hours on long journeys by plotting his next attack.***

Above: ***Digging up the Newall's garden. Dowser Brian Terriss was called in by police and informed them they were probably dealing with a murder inquiry.***

THEY DISCOVERED THE CLOTHING EXACTLY WHERE THE PSYCHIC HAD PREDICTED, BUT THE CORPSE HAD BEEN SWEPT DOWNSTREAM.

Opposite: ***Roderick Newall after pleading guilty to murdering his parents. The case is one of only a handful on record in which a dowser has been used to assist detectives.***

down and confessed that they were all true. He led them to the body, exactly as Dixie had described it.

HORRIFIC CRIME

One specialist in 'seeing' missing people after handling their personal items is Gerard Croiset. It was because of his accuracy in this field that he was asked by police to help pinpoint the whereabouts of a missing teenager.

Pat McAdam was hitchhiking home to Dumfries, Scotland, with her friend Hazel Campbell. They had been to an all-night party in Glasgow in February 1967. A lorry driver picked both of them up and drove Hazel to a point near her house. As the two girls bid each other goodnight, Hazel was not to know that she would never see her chum again.

Pat did not arrive home. Police interviewed the driver but the girl's body had not been found and they had nothing to go on. Enter psychic detective Gerard. He picked up Pat's Bible and after a brief meditation declared that the young girl had been killed.

He 'saw' a bridge from which her body had been thrown into a river. He went on to describe the house next to the bridge. It had an advertising hoarding on the side wall; in the garden was a car with no wheels and a wheelbarrow propped up against it. He believed the girl's body was caught underwater in the gnarled roots of trees on the riverbank. Her clothes were trapped so that she could not float to the surface. There were also clothes hanging in the branches.

The investigating officers already knew that the driver's lorry was often seen close to a bridge. When they searched the area that Gerard pinpointed, they found the house exactly as he had predicted. They also found the clothing but no body. The river had flooded and it was thought the corpse had disappeared downstream.

Pat's body was never found and her murderer never brought to book. However, ten years later a lorry driver was jailed for a similar, horrific crime: the multiple rape and murder of another poor woman. Although the police could never prove it, they suspected that the same man killed Pat.

A more unusual aid for spiritual detectives is a pendulum. Brian Terriss, a 56-year-old harbour worker from Guernsey, uses his powers as a dowser not to find water or metals but to find people. Brian searches for them by the ancient pendulum method, dangling the device over a map.

The pendulum swings and jerks until the missing person is located. If the person is alive and well, the pendulum swings round and round. If it goes dead then that is where the search for a body must begin.

Brian has only once been called in by police: when wealthy underwriter Nicholas Newall and his wife Elizabeth went missing on the neighbouring Channel Island of Jersey.

The dowser held some items belonging to the couple: a glove, a lipstick and pieces of clothing. When he held his pendulum over the missing pair's mementos, he came to the conclusion that they were both dead. Finding them was to prove much harder. He travelled to a bay in Jersey, where the couple's boat had been moored. He picked up vibes from his map, but a search failed to come up with the bodies.

Long after they were declared dead, their murdered bodies were found buried in woodlands. Both their sons were charged in connection with the killings.

On another occasion, again using his dowsing technique, Brian pinpointed the body of a dead seaman who had gone missing. Police searched the area but found nothing – yet the body turned up seven weeks later, exactly where Brian said it would be. Rescuers had failed to find it because seaweed had anchored it to the seabed.

How could he have known?

DAVID ICKE

He wanted to be world famous but a cruel and crippling illness put paid to his football career. Then David Icke discovered his alternative destiny: he was to be the saviour of the world.

As a soccer league hopeful David Icke would bellow at team defenders and mutter about the judgement of referees. In the chair as a top sports commentator he remarked on the finesse and form of snooker or football heroes of the day. Later, he became an outspoken champion of environmental issues, fighting passionately to free the Earth of its choking pollutants and other hazards. But none of these activities prepared the world for what was to come: David Icke as the son of God.

His astonishing declarations and further exploits as 'the chosen One' made him and his family the laughing stocks of the nation.

But how could a one-time goalie and happily married father of two have turned so spectacularly into a mystic messiah – collecting a curious female entourage in the process? To see him perform on the pitch, few would have guessed the baffling future he had in store.

As a teenager in Leicester he displayed some stunning sporting skills. It seemed he was going to realize every boy's dream of playing soccer for a top British club when he was signed as an apprentice by Coventry City at the age of only 15. Dexterous David Icke was the master of the goal mouth, diving and leaping to make exciting saves.

But soon his athletic prowess was hindered by a series of injuries. The joints in his knees and elbows would balloon with painful swellings. Doctors were unable to say what was causing the string of problems. Courageously, he overcame the discomfort to continue playing, but by the time he was 19 it was clear something was critically wrong.

He was devastated when rheumatoid arthritis was diagnosed before he celebrated his 20th birthday. It cruelly ended his promising career with Coventry City. He moved to lower league Hereford United and was part of the team which won promotion from the fourth to the third division. His agility finally deserted him when he was just 21. It was a personal disaster for Icke. The trauma was compounded when, without an income, he and his wife Linda were virtually evicted from their home. He had to make some hard decisions about his future – and fast.

HIS EXPRESSIVE EYES AND THE READY SMILE PLAYING AROUND HIS GENEROUS MOUTH ENSURED HIS APPEAL TO THE FEMALE AUDIENCE.

Above: *Icke was master of the goalmouth. He could make diving saves and leaping catches which left the crowds gasping in admiration. As a young keeper for top club Coventry, it seemed he might go all the way to the top and become goalie for the England team.*

Opposite: *He loved football. But he suffered a string of mystery injuries which hampered his performances. When rheumatoid arthritis was diagnosed it seemed Icke's glittering career had come to an end when he was aged only 21. It was the first hurdle of many in his life that he had to overcome.*

A HIGH FLIER

With his sporting pedigree he looked towards journalism, monitoring the action on the field instead of making it. Again it seemed certain he was headed for the big time.

From the launch-pad of his local newspaper in Leicester, Icke shot into sports broadcasting. He had a comfortably buoyant manner in front of the camera with expressive eyes and a ready smile playing around his generous mouth. His clean-cut good looks soon had him marked down as a high flier at the BBC.

When long-time anchorman Frank Bough left *Grandstand* it was thought by many that Icke would inherit the position. In fact, he did win the hot seat for a number of shows and proved himself a worthy recipient of the job.

But Icke had pushed noses out of joint at the BBC – which would spell his downfall. First, he refused to fly to international sports

Above: ***Icke became a first-class sports commentator. But above all he was a family man and didn't care who knew it. He preferred to stay at home with his wife Linda and their two children rather than jet off on overseas jaunts for work. His reluctance to leave them probably cost him a top job.***

Right: ***Linda was devoted to her husband, and he to her. She stuck by him through thick and thin and refused to believe the gossips who linked his name to that of another woman. Even when the shameful truth emerged, she stayed loyally at his side.***

events. He was, he told bosses, too terror-struck by aircraft travel to work abroad. When he was eventually sent overseas to cover the 1986 World Cup in Mexico he grumbled about the heat and the working conditions, to the chagrin of those left behind in London.

Even in Britain, he disliked travelling to events if it meant being parted from his wife Linda and children for too long. As a devoted father and husband, he had no time for the drinking and wild affairs that often accompany working trips, which further added to his reputation for being out of step. One producer summed it up. 'As a presenter he knocked everybody else I had into a cocked hat but he wasn't a prima donna and perhaps you have to be if you're going to make it to the top.'

FALL FROM GRACE

For the second time in his working life, he was no longer a golden boy and fell from grace. Rival Desmond Lynam was finally picked for the *Grandstand* job, leaving Icke frustrated and bitter. His brilliant career was reduced to fill-in spots from sporting events around the country. He was left reflecting on

a lost opportunity and facing a future of bit-part broadcasting.

To fill the void he decided to move to the Isle of Wight, where he had spent happy holidays as a boy. In 1984 Icke, Linda and their children Kerry, 9, and Gareth, 2, moved from Aylesbury to a flat in a Victorian mansion block at Ryde, Isle of Wight.

There he entered some quick-fire campaigns to establish himself in island life. First, there was the Steam Railway Society. Icke had always been fascinated by steam trains and longed to see them return to puff and wheeze along the disused tracks crossing his adopted home island. But he was allied to the slow-moving campaign to reintroduce old time railway services for less than a year.

He cast around for another interest and found a role in the Special Olympics for the Mentally Handicapped, but again his association with the organization was brief.

After that he flirted with politics, first joining the Liberal Democrats. He was proposed as a prospective MP for the island but dropped out after being short-listed.

Then Icke looked to the Green Party, which he considered a true reflection of his beliefs at the time. Within six months he became national spokesman for the Green Party. He even talked about being Britain's first Green MP. His passionate beliefs in installing sound environmental sense in the rest of the nation was set out in a book, *It doesn't have to be like this: Green Politics Explained* which sold 10,000 copies. But his abrasive style hallmarked by belligerence and barracking won him few friends. It was doubtful he would have won anything like the number of votes needed to make history and be Green in Parliament. The fact was, Icke never stood in an election to put his popularity to the test.

Residents in the close-knit community on the Isle of Wight finally lost faith in him following a noisy protest against the poll tax, the government's short-lived scheme to raise cash for local councils. The tax was about as popular and provocative as a fox in a hen house, so Icke found no shortage of supporters when he demonstrated against the introduction of the tax, pledging to go to jail rather than pay. When he defied the law, the BBC ended the dwindling number of contracts it had put his way. He was no longer a broadcaster but a live force in politics, if only for a brief spell.

But six months later it was revealed that he had paid up the money he owed, sidestepping the martyrdom – and discomfort – of a spell behind bars. Icke also faded from significance in the Green movement – which was still struggling to find a foothold in Britain's tightly run political scene. He finally resigned when he wrote to party leaders telling them of a book he was writing which would make his place in the party untenable.

Above: ***Icke became absorbed by green politics. The world was waking up to the long-term havoc being wreaked on the environment by mankind. It seemed the Green Party was at last winning popular support and even had a chance of entering Parliament. Icke was at the heart of the movement as national spokesperson for the party in Britain and was one of the four people regarded as the leaders of the group.***

Above: ***Icke won acclaim for his refusal to pay the poll tax, considered by many to be an unjust scheme. But his following dwindled when he quietly paid up rather than face jail.***

THE SAVIOUR OF THE EARTH

Behind the scenes, Icke had found a new cause which put everything else in the shade. He had been visiting medium and spiritual healer Betty Shine at her base in Brighton, ostensibly to find a cure for the arthritis which still plagued him.

But while he was visiting her for the third time in March 1990, she imparted some news from her contacts in the other world which made Icke sit up and listen. She communicated with a wise Chinese mandarin from the 12th century who was in the company of renowned philosopher Socrates. The message came back that Icke was in reality a healer who came to save Earth and was destined to be world famous. Before that could happen, he would have to abandon politics, the message relayed. For Icke, it was an eye-opener. His true purpose in life was at last exposed.

At the time Mrs Shine said she and Icke had undergone an amazing experience. 'I was giving him healing and suddenly this incredible person appeared and the whole room throbbed with the most tremendous power.

'It was just like a powerhouse and it shattered David. There were messages that he had got a job to do.'

Icke explained: 'Through Betty I received some astonishing revelations and predictions of fundamental importance to the future of humankind which set me on a journey of discovery that I would have found impossible to comprehend unless my path had crossed with hers.'

Aged 38, Icke felt the future of the world lay in his hands. He took his pivotal role seriously and set off around the world researching mystical religion, energy lines and the like.

At a Green Show held in the National Exhibition Centre in Birmingham, he met a group of people all committed to alternative beliefs, among them Deborah Shaw. Deborah was a teacher, born and brought up in Kenilworth, West Midlands. After qualifying, she taught deaf children in her home town until she moved to Calgary, Canada, on an exciting new contract.

In Canada, she had a plush apartment, a jeep and led a life-style which more befitted a wealthy executive than a humble teacher. That's because Deborah was a woman of means. Her shopowner father had died leaving a lump sum to his four children. Deborah was also a director of Toytown, a toyshop chain in the West Midlands.

After their initial meeting, Deborah wrote to Icke and invited him to Calgary. He went. It was there he became involved with women from a curious sect who took him to their hearts.

At a screening of a film about UFOs, he was introduced to Maia Trettler, a 48-year-old science teacher, who believes herself to be a reincarnation of St Francis of Assisi. Millions of years ago, she believes, she came from another planet and now she and fellow believers are known as the Brethren of the Flame.

She was known to dance naked with friends around a circle of stones in her garden and also to bow to the Sun.

Maia said of Icke later: "When he told me he was going to an Inca shrine in Peru I had to embrace him. After two minutes I said "I love you" and I gave him a psychic message. When David came back from Peru he asked me: "Did you know something passed between us when we embraced?"'

She went on: 'We are going to build a healing centre here in Calgary and I hope the entity you call David will play a major part. I've already put a £30,000 deposit on the land but I don't know where the money came from. Even the bank can't explain it. Sometimes it just seems to drop out of the sky. Everything we need will come the same way.'

In fact, the Brethren of the Flame is linked to the Church Universal and Triumphant. Its doctrine is based on the movement proclaimed in 1930 by engineer James Ballard after he had recounted a mountain top meeting with St Germain. Loosely explained, followers are urged to think and say positive, loving things to make the world a better place. It's often referred to as the 'I am' philosophy with its emphasis on phrases like 'I am feeling great'. When church leader Elizabeth Clare Prophet predicted the world would end in 1990, scores of believers trekked to her commune in Montana to seek refuge in a costly system of bomb shelters and defensive weapons.

Feeding off this intense spirituality, Icke and Deborah Shaw teamed up for trips across America and later around the world in the quest and thirst for greater understanding. While he was away Icke's father Beric died after a long illness and was buried before the wandering son – now apparently cured of his fear of flying – returned.

Deborah now changed her name to Mari Schawsun, explaining to friends she had always wanted to be called Maria after seeing *The Sound of Music*. And she seemed set to abandon the life she had made for herself in Canada in order to follow Icke across the globe. In March 1991 she was due to host a seminar she had planned meticulously for weeks previously, aimed at helping the deaf children she taught. Instead of turning up for the prestige event, she came to England to be at Icke's side. Thousands of miles away inside her Calgary apartment were her two cats who had given birth to five kittens and were left to fend for themselves until site managers broke in. After forcing an entry they found a ring of rocks on the floor.

A PROPHET OF DOOM

On his return to Britain David Icke gave a press conference to unveil his new persona. A stunned audience listened as he announced: 'I am the conveyor of new truths … a messenger of the great Godhead. I am here to warn the world of pending terrible disasters.'

Among his predictions were floods in Tayside, Mull of Kintyre, Ireland, Japan, Holland and Denmark, with tidal waves hitting Greece and southern Italy; earthquakes in China, Salzburg, Austria, Cuba, Mexico, Los Angeles, New York, Las Vegas and the Texan oilfields; volcanoes erupting in Washington, Italy, Martinique, Japan and Sicily; and tornadoes hitting

IT SEEMED THAT ICKE SINCERELY BELIEVED THAT THE FUTURE OF THE WORLD LAY IN HIS HANDS.

Opposite below: *Spiritual healer Betty Shine helped Icke to recover from some of the ravages of rheumatoid arthritis. On his third visit to her, she imparted some startling revelations to him.*

Below: *A cyclone caused devastation in Bangladesh in May 1991, claiming as many as 200,000 lives. Icke infuriated the aid agencies battling to do relief work among the injured and homeless there when he announced that the catastrophe proved he was a prophet.*

FOR ONCE THE JOURNALISTS WERE SPEECHLESS: THE FORMER SOCCER WHIZZ-KID WAS CLAIMING TO BE THE SON OF GOD.

Above: ***The Greek philosopher Plato, who revealed the teachings of Socrates. Betty Shine's communications with long-dead philosophers had a powerful influence on Icke.***

DAVID CLAIMED THAT A HIGHER FORCE HAD BROUGHT HIM AND MARI TOGETHER FOR SEX – AND THE PAIN WAS EXCRUTIATING!

Londonderry, Northern Ireland, and New Zealand. In addition, he forecast the collapse of the Channel Tunnel before its opening and the melting of the polar ice caps. Saddam Hussein was dead, he added for good measure, and later warned people not to wear black because of its damaging effects.

Revealing his strange predictions, Icke eventually returned to the soccer style parlance he knew his audience would understand. 'Nobody was more gobsmacked than me when my mission was revealed. Many people will not believe me. They have their free will. I'm laid-back about it.

'We have now reached a situation in time when our world is under threat. The Godhead itself has become imbalanced. The whole of creation could end. I am here, though, to tell you of these dangers. And there is still hope. Please believe, believe in the power of love. It's mankind's only escape.'

The world would end in 1997 unless more people issued loving thoughts and deeds, he insisted. Laudable his messages may have been, but they found little favour in the audience. The assembled journalists were virtually speechless at first and then began to openly ridicule Icke.

They found it bizarre beyond their wildest imagination that the former soccer whizz-kid was in front of them claiming to be the son of God.

A FAMILY AFFAIR

Even more strange was the appearance of Icke with his loyal wife Linda on one side and friend Mari on the other. Daughter Kerry, struggling to suppress nervous giggles, was also paraded for the press. All wore turquoise, Icke's chosen colour to symbolize love and wisdom.

Everyone wanted to know the extent of his relationship with Mari, labelled by Icke as the daughter of Christ. He would only declare: 'We have complementary energy patterns.'

Meanwhile, Linda would be known as Michaela, said Icke, being the earthly spirit of the Archangel.

His mother Barbara looked at all this askance. 'Any mother would be worried when her son starts behaving like this. I don't know what's happened to him, he never used to be religious.'

His brother Paul went further. 'Some of the things he has said sound totally far-fetched, suggesting he's flipped his lid and gone round the bend.'

As for Icke, he practically cut them off from his new spiritual life, telling them only they would understand more if they read his book.

Eyebrows were raised even further when it was clear Mari was living with Icke and his wife in their Isle of Wight flat between their jaunts around the world.

Within months, a massive cyclone devastated Bangladesh, killing 200,000 people. Icke claimed it was proof of his predictions. His comments provoked a furious response from British charities who helped mop up the after-effects of the catastrophe.

A spokesman for the Red Cross pointed out: 'Bangladesh is extremely disaster-prone and therefore it is very easy to predict cyclones there.'

Icke was then drawn to Britain's mysterious corn circles. The circular patterns which appear in farmer's fields are thought by some to be created by energy forces although others believe them to be an elaborate hoax.

After waiting until sightseers had left the circle which appeared in Alton Barnes, Wiltshire, in July 1991, he emerged from his car in customary turquoise tracksuit and ran around the circle in an apparently trance-like state, in the company of a woman.

By now the public were cautiously intrigued by Icke – not that many were rushing to sign up for his newly expounded religion. Most of all, they were compelled and perplexed to know what could cause an apparently stable man to act so weirdly. Was he mad or simply the centre of a publicity bonanza?

When he appeared on the TV chat show *Wogan*, the BBC received 241 calls in protest. Just 14 objected on the grounds of blasphemy. The rest thought it was quite wrong to allow someone showing sure signs of mental illness to appear on TV. And they weren't alone. Psychologists called in by newspapers were quick to diagnose Icke's mental state as being near collapse. Former colleagues struggled to find words to explain his outlandish behaviour.

People also freely speculated about Icke's relationship with heiress Mari Schawsun. A

Sunday newspaper revealed the pair shared a king-sized bed during one of their foreign visits. His wife, who stayed at home while they went around the world, insisted there was nothing between them. Savings were paying for the family's bills and the trips abroad, she told inquiring reporters. Any inner torment at the activities of her husband of more than 20 years was cleverly disguised.

Later she told a newspaper: 'I would love to have gone with them but we didn't have the money. There were also two children to look after – they have always come first.'

And she revealed how David finally admitted to illicit nights of passion.

'David was absolutely distraught, he couldn't bear to look at me. But Mari was cool. She just said, in a matter-of-fact way: "We thought you knew."'

David told her how a higher force brought him and Mari together for sex.

'I can't remember anything except the power of the energies that came through. The energy was unbelievable, like swhoosh, right through the top of my head. When Mari and I were doing this it was as if I was not really there in the room. I was floating somewhere above, almost as if I was on the ceiling.

'I kept saying: "No way." I didn't want any part of that. I had never been unfaithful to Lin and the pain was excruciating. All I saw was her face. No one could love his wife more, everybody who knows me knows that. That woman is absolutely everything to me.

'At times I have felt so guilty I felt like walking into the sea and disappearing.'

Together, the pair picked up the pieces of shattered trust. During lengthy seafront strolls they vowed they would never part despite the affair. Somehow Linda found the strength to accept her rival's presence under the same roof.

'People will say I am mad or blind. But I am neither, Mari said it was a triangle that would last for ever but in my heart I knew she was wrong. We did not have rows even when it was all in the open.

'Part of me was thinking all the time, this is for the greater good and if we don't do it we might harm the Universe. The other part, a down-to-earth Midlands wife, was saying

Above: ***At a press conference, journalists looked on open-mouthed as Icke declared he was a mystic messenger who had come to warn them of impending doom. Beside him were his wife Linda, daughter Kerry – and heiress Deborah Shaw, otherwise known as Mari Shawsun. All wore turquoise, the colour nominated by Icke to represent love and wisdom.***

ICKE REMAINS CONVINCED THAT HIS PROPHECIES WILL COME TRUE UNLESS MORE PEOPLE FOLLOW HIS TEACHINGS.

Above: ***Despite their difficulties, Icke, his wife Linda and their children remain as close as ever. They are still committed to their strong spiritual beliefs. After Icke's affair was revealed, Linda said: 'Part of me was thinking all the time, this is for the greater good and if we don't do it we might harm the Universe.'***

to herself: "I wish she would pack her bags and go back to Canada."

'I have always been totally sure of David's love for me. There was never any suggestion of a romance despite what Mari has said.'

A FINAL GOODBYE

But it was with relief that she greeted the news that Mari was moving out. As autumn dawned she helped pack the bags and said a final goodbye to 'the other woman'.

For two months life in the Icke household bore some semblance of normality. Then came a telephone call which threatened to throw their new-found happiness into chaos again. Mari said she was having David's baby.

Both David and Linda cared little what people thought about their activities. They only became concerned if the scorn and insults from others were aimed at their children.

David only spoke out about the arrival of Mari's child, called Rebecca, when he was accused of failing to provide the necessary financial support. It was, he asserted, patent nonsense to suggest he would turn his back on any child of his. He was even willing to bring up the child himself if that was what the mother wanted.

With the furore over Mari's baby still in the air, Linda became pregnant too. She was sensitive to suggestions that, at 42, she became pregnant in a tit-for-tat revenge on her rival which would keep her husband by her side.

'It was nothing to do with cementing our relationship because, despite all that has happened it has never been rocky. It sort of happened and I couldn't be happier.'

She gave birth to a boy at the start of 1993.

As for David Icke, his days are now spent reading the mountains of mail that come his way after writing four books, among them *The Truth Vibrations*, much of the mail being supportive.

He remains convinced more and more people will follow his teachings. As he writes in *The Truth Vibrations*: 'I am well aware of what the reaction to this book will be. The people reading it will fall into three main categories: those who laugh; those who condemn and those for whom it will change their lives forever ... And with every month and year that passes, the latter group will grow and grow until it is the largest.'

At weekends, he plays football again, either with his elder son Gareth or for a local team where he made his comeback two years ago.

Spiritual healing has improved his arthritis sufficiently for him to take his place in goal once more. Supporters were quick to test their wit on him. 'We want to make a profit, not sign one,' yelled one. 'No good on the cross, eh?' roared another. But Icke had enough commonsense to practice what he preached. He turned the other cheek.